Summer Delights

Summer Delights

**Noël
Richardson**

Whitecap Books
Vancouver/Toronto

Edited by Elaine Jones
Interior design by Carolyn Deby

Line drawings by J. Ward-Harris

Typography by CompuType, Vancouver, B.C., Canada

Printed and bound in Canada by
Friesen Printers, Altona, Manitoba

Canadian Cataloguing in Publication Data

Richardson, Noël, 1937-
    Summer delights

    Includes index.
    ISBN 1-895-099-47-1

    1. Cookery (Herbs).   2. Herb gardening.
I. Ward-Harris, Joan.   II. Title.
 TX819.H4R53 1991   641.6'57   C91-091080-4

The first edition of this book was packaged and produced by David Robinson.

Contents

To my mother,
Dolly Richardson,
who sent me at an early age
to pick mint for the new potatoes
and to Andrew Yeoman,
who created our herb farm

Introduction

On the eve of its third printing, I am writing a new introduction for the revised edition of *Summer Delights*. As I write this, I am sitting at the dining room table gazing at the white-frosted winter garden, worrying about the two little bay trees that have survived three years in the garden but now look miserable. I am also making New Year's herb resolutions for the spring and summer, promising myself to plant more opal basil so I can have bouquets as well as pink basil vinegar, to put more Corsican mint in the cracks of the old brick path, to plant more lavender, and to sow more nasturtiums for salads.

In 1979, we moved to Ravenhill Herb Farm in Saanichton on Vancouver Island and started our own herb farm. For the first two years, we planted seeds and plants, read vast numbers of gardening and cookbooks and experimented daily. By the summer of 1981, we thought we had enough plants to sell some of our herbs, so we contacted a few restaurants and offered them fresh-cut herbs. In addition, we self-published a little booklet, *Summer Delights*, a precursor to the first edition of this book.

Since then, my experience with herbs has deepened and widened. I read more herbals, visit more herb gardens, continue experimenting with herbs in my cooking, and I have written a second cookbook called *Winter Pleasures: Herbs and Comfort Cooking*, which focuses on winter cooking and preserving herbs for winter. I have also begun to realize how herbs have been a comforting companion for humans since the earliest times, when the first women began to gather wild greens to add to their diet. These green plants were especially important if the hunters were unsuccessful in the hunt. Slowly, over the centuries, the use of herbs wove its way into many areas of life: our food, medicine, religious rituals, scenting and decoration of our homes, and, of course, our gardens.

In my travels I have found herb gardens in such varied places as the heart of London, on the island of Bermuda, Malibu Beach and in New York City. Each time I come upon a neat lavender hedge, a sturdy rosemary bush or even a patch of wild fennel in a vacant lot, my heart leaps in a happy response: "Ah, there you are my friends."

I cannot imagine living without herbs, and sometimes when I look into the future, I see myself, an elderly lady with a tiny cottage and a small patio with pots and pots of herbs inside and outside of my house, and I am pottering about tending my herbal companions.

One does not need a vast garden to grow herbs: a balcony, a patio or a kitchen window sill can provide space for many pots of herbs. In fact, I could begin a campaign for only edible houseplants, and people could happily fill their houses with bay trees, rosemarys, sages, winter savorys and basil, and double their plant pleasure, for you can eat the leaves as well as admire the foliage.

In the last five years, I have been giving herbal cooking classes in the kitchen at Ravenhill Farm. The classes usually include lunch or dinner, and I started to make herbal desserts and to bake cakes and cookies with herbs. My dessert experiments were greeted with enthusiasm, and so this new edition of the book has an additional chapter using herbs in desserts and baking.

Summer Delights has elicited a warm response. I have had many telephone calls and letters from people who said the book had inspired them to begin an herb garden and start using herbs in their cooking. Fifteen years ago, I was an herbal novice who only had mint, chives and parsley in my garden, and dozens of bottles of dried herbs in my kitchen. Most of the jars are gone and the garden is now full of an amazing selection of plants to flavor our food.

My herbal journey has been fascinating and has enlivened my life and led me down many paths. The connection with the people who have visited the farm on summer Sundays in the past few years has enriched our lives and extended our knowledge of herbs and gardens. Passionate cooks, professional chefs, herb farmers, landscapers and gardeners have come to the farm, sharing their enthusiasm, knowledge, flowers and cuttings.

Growing and cooking with herbs can be satisfying in so many ways and on so many levels. There is the flavor they add to our food, the addition of vitamins and their digestive qualities, the visual and decorative effect on the dinner plate, in the garden or as a wreath on the door, and the feeling of historical continuity which adds an important dimension to our lives. Tending of herb gardens has been going on for centuries, and to be occupied in such an atavistic but gentle and useful pastime can only be good for us and the earth.

I would like to thank my husband, Andrew Yeoman, whose careful growing of the herbs this past twelve years has been the springboard for my cookbooks, and the basis of our wonderful life at Ravenhill Farm. He has written the following section on growing herbs, as well as the growing instructions for each herb in individual chapters.

Gardens, Great and Small

The nineteen herbs in this book are not just a cook's delight, but also a gardener's delight. They can survive a wide range of light, soil and moisture conditions. They can all be placed together in one bed in your garden or scattered around, but we have found that much greater leaf production is possible if the herbs in this book are separated into three groups: those suited to the vegetable garden, those suited to the rock garden, and those suited to the flower garden.

The vegetable garden herbs include basil, chervil, chives, cilantro, dill, fennel, horseradish, sweet marjoram, parsley, summer savory, sorrel and tarragon. These herbs require a soil rich in organic material, and regular watering in dry weather—the same conditions as the vegetables in your garden.

Among the vegetable garden herbs, there are the perennials and the annuals. The perennials—fennel, horseradish, sorrel and tarragon—may be grouped together, as they develop massive root systems and can stay in one place for at least four years. Chives, too, are a perennial, but they need to be dug up and divided every other year if maximum leaf production is desired. The annuals—chervil, cilantro, dill and summer savory, as well as basil and sweet marjoram (perennials grown as annuals)—are resown each year.

The rock garden, or foundation planting herbs include French or hardy marjoram, oregano, rosemary, sage, winter savory and English and lemon thyme. These herbs require little in the way of organic material in the soil and, once established, require infrequent watering in dry weather. They are all perennials.

Several of the vegetable and rock garden herbs can be grown in the flower garden. Flower garden herbs have forms, leaf coloring and flowers that add to the beauty of your garden. They include basil, chives, fennel, lemon balm, lovage, mint (if roots are confined), sage and tarragon. These herbs appreciate a soil that is moderately rich in organic material and require weekly watering in dry weather.

Soil

If your soil is compacted, infertile or has a high clay content, it should be dug over or tilled as deeply as possible before planting a herb garden. Where soil is thin (less than one foot / 30 cm to bedrock, sand or clay) or where water drainage is poor, the use of raised beds will greatly improve the quality of the herbs and, in some cases, be essential for their survival.

If your soil has little or no organic material in it, then the addition of compost, aged manure, leaf mold, sawdust (not cedar) or peat moss is important. Basil, chives, parsley and sorrel do best in rich soil, but marjoram, oregano, rosemary, sage, winter savory and English and lemon thyme need only minor amounts of organic material and can be set back by the use of too strong compost or aged manure.

Most herbs grow best in nonacidic, limy soils. If your soil is acidic, ground limestone, dolomite or crushed shells should be added to your herb garden when herbs are planted and as a top dressing to the soil every winter. Wood ash and bone meal have the same effect, but they should be used in moderation and mixed well with the soil.

Fertilizer

Provided that soil and moisture requirements have been met for the three groups of herbs, regular fertilization is necessary only for basil, chives, parsley and sorrel, and only when plants are being heavily picked. Fertilize according to directions given in the individual chapters.

Light and Shade

While it is true that most herbs grow better in sunny positions, many herbs produce well in semishady spots and can even produce tasty leaves without direct sunlight. The herbs that require the most sunshine are the aromatic, shrubby perennials: marjoram, oregano, rosemary, sage, winter savory and English and lemon thyme. Herbs that perform reasonably well with only three or four hours of direct sunlight are basil, chives, horseradish, lemon balm, lovage, sorrel and tarragon. Herbs that will grow on northern exposures without direct sunlight, provided that indirect light is strong and the soil is kept moist but not soggy, are chervil, cilantro, dill, fennel, mint and parsley. Herbs growing under these conditions, however, will probably not set seeds.

The Spacing Myth

Spacing distances detailed in most gardening books and on seed packages refer to the space required for a large plant in presumably ideal conditions. Gardeners whose space is limited, who are growing herbs in containers or under cold frames, or who want to speed up the first cutting of herbs grown from seed can experiment with much closer spacings.

Close-spacing cultivation is suitable for annuals like chervil, cilantro, dill and summery savory, and also for perennials grown like annuals from seed, such as basil, fennel, lovage, sweet and hardy marjoram, oregano, sage, sorrel and English thyme (not lemon thyme). While this method is best suited to growing herbs from seed, it can also be used with young plants bought from nurseries.

Close-spacing cultivation requires a soil that is fine-textured and porous and it requires good drainage. The closer the spacing, the greater the care needed in watering and fertilizing. If seeds are broadcast rather than sown in rows, the first cutting will be greater per square foot, but weeding, watering and fertilizing will be more difficult with each additional cutting and the yield of second and third cuttings may be reduced. To prevent this, broadcast-sow, then, after the first or second cutting, create rows by hoeing or hand thinning. Water with a very fine spray and soak between the rows. Fertilize with quarter-strength liquid 20-20-20 fertilizer two weeks after germination, increasing it to half-strength when young plants are growing strongly. Cutting can start when plants are 3 to 4 inches (7.5 to 10 cm) tall. Plants should be pulled up after three to four cuttings or when they do not respond to fertilizer. Close-spacing cultivation produces a mild-flavored herb leaf that is ideal for salads and garnishes.

Extending the Season

Rigid cold frames, or some form of plastic-covered hoop frames, are invaluable for extending the growing season in the spring and fall, as well as for overwintering many herbs. Seeds such as chervil, cilantro, dill, fennel, parsley, summer savory and sorrel can be grown under plastic in early spring. In the spring, cold frames can be moved over established plants of chives, fennel, parsley, sorrel and tarragon in order to bring forward the first cutting by two or three weeks.

Light plastic frames, if well anchored, are suitable for late spring, summer and early fall use, but heavy, fixed cold frames are necessary for winter. Young plants can be moved to a cold frame in early fall, but some plants, like chervil and parsley, are best sown in an uncovered cold frame in late summer or covered in fall. Cold frames are, in addition, excellent places to overwinter container plants.

Container Gardening on Balconies, Steps and Patios

All the herbs in this book can be grown in containers and all of them are easy to care for through the spring, summer and fall. Six herbs, fennel, horseradish (for leaves only), lovage, sage, sorrel and tarragon, are excellent container plants when young, but develop such huge root systems after the first year that they outgrow all but the largest containers. To grow herbs in containers, the soil should be a mix of 50 percent light soil, 25 percent perlite, 25 percent sand, plus a little peat moss and ground limestone or dolomite. Prepackaged mixes from garden centers are fine, but they may need additional perlite or sand to improve the drainage, as well as 2 tablespoons (30 mL) ground limestone or dolomite, or oyster shell, for each 6-inch (15-cm) diameter pot. All containers should have drainage holes and a layer of pebbles covering the bottom. Before filling each pot with soil, put a layer of newspaper over the pebbles to prevent the soil mixture from sifting through the pebbles.

Fertilizing container-grown herbs depends on the amount and quality of growth: there are no hard and fast rules, only general guidelines. Organic fish fertilizer and liquid 20-20-20 fertilizer are both good for container-grown herbs. Most herbs, if overwintered outside, benefit from a dose of half-strength fish fertilizer in the early spring when strong growth is underway. Fertilizer at this time replaces some of the nitrogen washed away during the winter. Heavy nitrogen-users, such as basil, chives, parsley and sorrel, need fertilizer every week if the plants are being heavily picked. Chervil, cilantro, dill, fennel, lovage, sweet marjoram, oregano, sage and summer savory also need weekly doses of fertilizer if the plants are young, grown close together and heavily harvested. When the plants are more mature, using fertilizer every two weeks will probably be enough during the growing and cutting season. As the root masses grow to fill the containers, more frequent, but weaker doses of fertilizer should be used. If full-strength fertilizer is being used, it is important to water the plants first. We usually use fertilizer at one-half the strength advised on the package. Plants that have been fertilized frequently for a few months will benefit from being soaked for 10 minutes in a bucket of water to dissolve away any salts that may not have been used by the roots.

Southern, eastern and western exposures are good for almost all the herbs in this book, but the containers need some shade to prevent overheating in the midday and afternoon sun. Chervil is really the only exception to this rule. It needs shade from strong, direct sunlight all summer. Those with north-facing balconies need not despair, however. It should be possible to grow excellent leaves of chervil, cilantro, dill, fennel, mint and parsley.

We hope that this general cultivation advice, and the more specific comments given in individual chapters, will enable readers to successfully grow herbs in their garden or on balconies, steps or patios. And we hope the herbs in this book bring as much *delight* to your summers as they have to ours at Ravenhill Herb Farm. Experiment in growing and cooking with herbs, as the possibilities and combinations are endless. That is why growing herbs and cooking with them is such a fascinating source of pleasure, to the gardener and cook alike.

Basil

For the imaginative cook, the pleasures of basil increase every year. Its rich, exotic flavor and perfume add new dimensions to vegetables, pasta dishes, fish and chicken. The combinations are endless. The first time that a child is served pesto, ignore the protest and you will probably find that a pesto addiction will develop. You may discover that you do not want to eat fresh tomatoes without chopped basil on top; for us, this is one of the greatest pleasures of summer. Basil is a favorite herb of Italian, Provençal and Greek cooks.

Growing

*B*asil is a tropical perennial grown as an annual in temperate latitudes. Sow it indoors under good light in early spring, and pot up one month later. Plants can be put out in the garden under plastic tunnels or cloches one month after that. If there is good ventilation on sunny days, plants will benefit from plastic tunnels until early summer. The most common cause of failure is placing the plants out too early without adequate protection.

The only insect problem that we have had with basil is flea beetles when first setting out plants in the ground. This is easily countered by small amounts of rotenone dust.

If plants have not started to bush out when 6 inches (15 cm) high, the central growth point should be pinched. Soil for basil needs to be rich, and plants will benefit from liquid fish fertilizer every two weeks in the heavy picking period. If grown in fast-draining soils, watering is necessary every two or three days in dry weather.

Wide-leafed basil carries the greatest weight of leaves and has an excellent flavor. Small-leafed basil is preferred by some cooks and makes a more attractive plant for containers or the flower garden. Basil can easily be grown as a container plant in the summer, but does not usually yield as much as in the garden.

Basil can be dug up and brought inside in early fall to extend the season. To grow basil successfully through the winter, it is necessary to use grow lamps, and to have normal house temperatures and high humidity.

Basil Butter

Place a dollop of this savory butter on barbecued hamburgers, steaks, lamb chops or fish. Basil Butter keeps in the refrigerator for several weeks or it can be frozen.

4 Tbsp. (60 mL) chopped basil leaves

2 cloves garlic, peeled and chopped

1/2 cup (125 mL) softened butter

freshly ground black pepper

Put all ingredients in a blender or food processor. Process until smooth and chill in a small crock.

Basil Oil

Use this fragrant oil for salad dressings or drizzle it over pizzas, barbecued meats and fish. Makes 2 cups (500 mL).

4-6 Tbsp. (60-90 mL) chopped basil leaves

2 cups (500 mL) olive or vegetable oil

Put basil in a blender or food processor with a little oil and blend or process for a few seconds. Add remaining oil and blend well. Put in a sterilized bottle and seal tightly. Shake occasionally. If sealed well, it will keep for several months.

Tomato and Basil Salad

When I think of August, I think of this famous but simple salad. I have it for lunch almost every day while fresh tomatoes and basil are abundant. Serves 4.

6 ripe tomatoes, sliced

3 Tbsp. (45 mL) olive or vegetable oil

1 Tbsp. (15 mL) wine or balsamic vinegar

freshly ground black pepper

1/2 cup (125 mL) finely chopped basil leaves

Lay tomato slices on a platter. Mix oil, vinegar and pepper together in a cup. Sprinkle chopped basil over tomato slices. Pour oil and vinegar mixture over top.

Let salad sit for 30 minutes so that the flavors can be absorbed by the tomatoes. This is a good side dish for salmon or any barbecued meat.

Gazpacho Summer Soup

There are many versions of this quick, cold soup, so don't hesitate to vary the ingredients and experiment with the recipe. It makes a good supper with a loaf of crusty bread. Serves 4.

10 medium-ripe tomatoes, peeled and chopped

2-4 cloves garlic, peeled and chopped

4 Tbsp. (60 mL) olive oil

3 Tbsp. (45 mL) white wine vinegar

dash of hot-pepper sauce

freshly ground black pepper

2 green peppers, seeded and diced

1 cucumber, peeled and diced

4 stalks celery, diced

2 medium onions, diced

4 Tbsp. (60 mL) finely chopped basil leaves

2 eggs, hard-boiled and chopped

2 cups (250 mL) croutons

Process tomatoes, garlic, oil and vinegar in a blender or food processor. Add a dash of hot-pepper sauce and blend. Season with pepper. Chill mixture in the refrigerator for 1 hour to increase the flavor. Just before serving, add diced green peppers, celery, cucumber and onions. Add basil and chill once again.

Serve in chilled bowls with two side dishes of chopped hard-boiled eggs and croutons, to sprinkle over the soup before eating.

Tomato, Basil and Mozzarella Salad

Combine pungent basil, mild mozzarella and juicy tomatoes drizzled with olive oil, for a delicious, nutritious and quick lunch. Italians have been eating it for hundreds of years. Serves 2-3.

3-4 ripe tomatoes, sliced

1/2 lb. (250 g) fresh mozzarella cheese, sliced

4 Tbsp. (60 mL) finely chopped basil leaves

3 Tbsp. (45 mL) olive or vegetable oil

1 Tbsp. (15 mL) wine or balsamic vinegar

freshly ground black pepper

Overlap slices of tomato and mozzarella cheese on a flat serving platter. Sprinkle chopped basil over tomatoes and cheese. Mix oil, vinegar and pepper together in a cup. Pour oil and vinegar mixture over top. Let salad sit for 30 minutes before serving, so that the flavors can be absorbed.

Pesto Sauce

This startling green sauce, which can be made so quickly and easily in 4-5 minutes, has become all the rage. We do not think this trend will fade. Instead, pesto sauce will become a summer classic, as it is in Italy. During basil season, we keep a jar of pesto sauce on hand in the refrigerator at all times. We think of it as a kind of Italian peanut butter! It is wonderful on toast or crackers, or served as a dip with hors d'oeuvres. You can put pesto sauce on hot pasta, on hot vegetables, or on barbecued meats. When using it with hot pasta, put a little extra Parmesan cheese on top. This basic recipe for pesto sauce can be altered: increase the garlic if you like; add parsley if you are short of basil; substitute sunflower seeds or walnuts for pine nuts. Also, you can use Romano cheese in combination with the Parmesan cheese. Experiment with this recipe until you get the pesto sauce you like. Serves 4.

2 cups (500 mL) freshly washed, firmly packed basil leaves

2-4 cloves garlic, peeled and crushed

1/2 cup (125 mL) olive or vegetable oil

3 Tbsp. (45 mL) pine nuts

1 cup (250 mL) freshly grated Parmesan cheese

Put basil and garlic in a blender or food processor. Pour in oil and process until smooth. Add pine nuts and process for a few seconds. Stir in Parmesan cheese. If sauce is too thick, add more oil or a few tablespoons (mL) of pasta or vegetable-cooking water.

If you are not using the pesto sauce right away, store it in a sterilized jar in the refrigerator with a skim of oil on top and cover with plastic wrap. Pesto sauce will keep like this for several weeks. To freeze pesto sauce for the winter, process basil, garlic and oil and freeze in plastic cartons. To use, thaw slowly at room temperature and then add pine nuts and Parmesan cheese before serving. Do not heat pesto, as it turns very dark and is unappetizing.

Broiled Cod with Pesto

Cod is an often-unappreciated fish. It is very adaptable and is a good blank canvas for a cook. This recipe is equally good with halibut. Serve it with rice or parsleyed new potatoes. Serves 4.

2 cups (500 mL) freshly washed, firmly packed basil leaves

2 cloves garlic, peeled and crushed

1/2 cup (125 mL) olive oil

2 ripe tomatoes, peeled and chopped

2 Tbsp. (30 mL) olive oil

4 anchovy fillets

freshly ground black pepper

4 cod steaks, approximately 1 inch (2.5 cm) thick

olive oil (to brush on steaks)

To make the pesto, put basil and garlic in blender or food processor. Pour in oil and process until smooth, then set aside.

Sauté tomatoes in oil in a skillet for 5 minutes. Add anchovies to skillet and season with pepper. Simmer over low heat while cod is being broiled/grilled.

Preheat oven to broil/grill. Brush cod steaks with oil and broil/grill in oven on a rack, 3-4 inches (7.5-10 cm) from the element, for 4-5 minutes per side.

Put the cod on a warm serving platter. Stir pesto sauce into tomato mixture. Pour this sauce over the cod and serve.

Roast Chicken with Pesto Sauce

This makes a good outdoor summer meal. Roast, as usual, 1 large roasting chicken or 2–3 fryers or several Cornish game hens. This can be done earlier in the day. Before dinner, make a double batch of pesto sauce (page 7). Carve chicken onto plates and put a dollop of pesto sauce on each serving. Serve with a green salad and French bread for a cool meal on a hot summer's day.

Sautéed Sole with Basil and Parmesan

The rich, complex flavors of basil and Parmesan make everyday sole fillets into a company dish. Serves 2.

2 large fillets of sole

4 Tbsp. (60 mL) butter

freshly ground black pepper

4 Tbsp. (60 mL) finely chopped basil leaves

3/4 cup (175 mL) freshly grated Parmesan cheese

4 Tbsp. (60 mL) chicken or fish stock, or clam nectar

Quickly sauté sole in butter in a skillet on both sides until browned. Season with pepper. Mix basil and Parmesan cheese together in a bowl and sprinkle over sole. Pour chicken or fish stock around sole in skillet. Simmer over low heat for 8-10 minutes until cheese has melted and fish has cooked.

Put on a warm serving platter and garnish with sprigs of parsley and basil. This recipe can also be baked in a 350°F (180°C) oven for 12-15 minutes until the cheese melts and the fish flakes.

Quick Tomato and Basil Sauce

A versatile, quick sauce to use on pasta, plain fried chicken or meat loaf. The anchovies and basil give it a South of France flavor. Serves 4.

2 or more cloves garlic, peeled and crushed

2 Tbsp. (30 mL) olive oil

6 ripe tomatoes, peeled and chopped

6 anchovy fillets (optional)

4 Tbsp. (60 mL or more finely chopped basil leaves

freshly ground black pepper

Sauté garlic in oil in a skillet for 1 minute. Add tomatoes and anchovies. Cover and simmer for 10 minutes. Add basil. Simmer for an additional 2 minutes.

Serve hot or refrigerate for later use. You may want to add 2 Tbsp. (30 mL) finely chopped Italian parsley and 2 Tbsp. (30 mL) finely chopped oregano to this recipe.

Creamy Basil Dressing

A pale green, smooth dressing that is very good on tomatoes, salads, shrimp, or used as a dip for vegetables. It is quick and easy to make in a blender or food processor. Makes 2 cups (500 mL).

1/4 cup (50 mL) freshly washed, firmly packed basil leaves

1 cup (250 mL) mayonnaise

1/2 cup (125 mL) sour cream

3 green onions, chopped

1 clove garlic, peeled and crushed

3 Tbsp. (45 mL) white wine vinegar

2 Tbsp. (30 mL) chopped tarragon

2 Tbsp. (30 mL) chopped chives

1 tsp. (5 mL) Worcestershire sauce

1/2 tsp. (2 mL) dry mustard

freshly ground black pepper

Combine all ingredients in a blender or food processor until smooth. Chill until ready to serve. This dressing will keep in the refrigerator for several days.

Three Cheese Pasta Sauce with Herbs

A herbed version of Alfredo Sauce that is creamy and rich, so I serve it with a simple, tart salad for contrast. Serves 4.

1 cup (250 mL) whipping cream

2 Tbsp. (30 mL) finely chopped shallots

1/4 cup (50 mL) cream cheese

1/4 cup (50 mL) crumbled blue cheese

1/4 cup (50 mL) freshly grated Parmesan cheese

1/4 cup (50 mL) finely chopped basil leaves

1/4 cup (50 mL) chopped chives

freshly ground black pepper

1 lb. (500 g) cooked pasta

Put cream and shallots in a saucepan. Simmer over medium heat for several minutes. Add the cheeses and stir with a whisk until well blended. Remove saucepan from heat. Add basil and chives and season with pepper.

Spoon over the hot cooked pasta and toss together well. Serve immediately. At the table, sprinkle with extra freshly grated Parmesan cheese.

Soupe au Pistou

Pistou is a French variant of pesto. This is a perfect soup to make in the summer when fresh vegetables are so bountiful. You can alter the vegetables depending on what is at the market or in your garden. Serves 6-8.

2 leeks, washed and finely chopped (use only the white part)

1 medium onion, finely chopped

6 Tbsp. (90 mL) vegetable oil

5-6 cups (1.25-1.5 L) cold water

2 carrots, peeled and diced

1 cup (250 mL) cooked white navy beans, or 1 can
  (14 fl.oz./398 mL) white navy beans

freshly ground black pepper

4 ripe tomatoes, peeled and chopped

2 cups (500 mL) chopped green beans

2 cups (500 mL) finely chopped zucchini

1/2 cup (125 mL) macaroni pieces

Pistou Basil Sauce (recipe follows)

Sauté leeks and onions in oil in a saucepan until limp. Add water, carrots and navy beans to saucepan and bring to a boil. Season with pepper. Reduce heat to low and simmer for 45-50 minutes. Add tomatoes, green beans and zucchini and simmer for an additional 20-30 minutes. Add macaroni and simmer for 10-15 minutes more, until tender.

Serve in heated bowls with Pistou Basil Sauce. Place a bowl of the sauce in the middle of the table so everyone can help themselves to a dollop of sauce in their soup. For a complete meal, serve with a loaf of crusty bread and a robust red wine.

Pistou Basil Sauce

1 cup (250 mL) freshly washed, firmly packed basil leaves

3-4 cloves garlic, peeled and crushed

1/4 cup (50 mL) olive or vegetable oil

1/2 cup (125 mL) freshly grated Parmesan cheese

Combine all ingredients in a blender or food processor until smooth.

Basil Vinegar

This is one of our favorite vinegars for dressings. We make it with large-leafed basil, tiny-leafed basil and opal basil, which makes a beautiful, pink-rosy vinegar. You may want to add a clove of garlic to give your vinegar extra zip.

Wash and sterilize your bottles. Put several sprigs of fresh basil in each bottle. Bring white wine vinegar to a boil in a saucepan. Fill bottles with vinegar. Cap and store in a cool, dark place for several weeks before using. The flavor will increase. This method can be used for all herb vinegars.

Baked Potato with Pesto

A spoonful of pesto perks up most vegetables and is particularly good on baked potatoes. Bake your potatoes the usual way. Serve with a dollop of pesto sauce and sprinkle with some freshly grated Parmesan cheese. This is almost a meal in itself and is a refreshing change from the usual sour cream topping.

Chervil

hervil is a delicate herb with an anise licorice flavor. It goes well with egg and cheese dishes. Its flavor is subtle, not at all overpowering, and it combines well with other herbs such as chives and parsley. Do not cook chervil too much; its flavor is best if you add it at the last minute.

Growing

*C*hervil is an annual that can be sown outside in early spring and again in late summer, for a second crop. Chervil likes fairly rich soil, frequent watering in dry weather and shade from the summer sun. Fall crops can be extended into the winter with the use of cold frames. It is a good container plant. If sown in pots in early fall and brought in before heavy frost, chervil will do well in a cool greenhouse. House or apartment temperatures are normally too high for this delicate, ferny herb.

Scrambled Eggs with Chervil

This is what the cook makes for supper when energy is low. Chervil and eggs pair wonderfully, and served with a salad, it's a delicious, easy meal. Serves 4.

8 large eggs

freshly ground black pepper

2 Tbsp. (30 mL) butter

2 Tbsp. (30 mL) half-and-half cream

4 Tbsp. (60 mL) finely chopped chervil, reserving 1 Tbsp. (15 mL) for garnish

Beat eggs lightly in a bowl. Season with pepper. Melt butter in a skillet and pour in eggs. Cook very slowly over low heat, scraping the bottom of the pan so that the eggs do not set. When almost done, stir in cream and chervil. Eggs should be creamy and moist, not dry. Serve on thin slices of whole-wheat bread or toast. Garnish with reserved chervil.

Chervil Sauce

A useful white sauce that can be served with many things: eggs, fish, chicken, or vegetables such as zucchini or summer squash. A reliable standby for the cook, it can also be made with tarragon. Serves 4.

1 cup (250 mL) half-and-half cream

1/2 cup (125 mL) finely chopped chervil leaves, reserving the whole chervil stems

2 Tbsp. (30 mL) butter

1 Tbsp. (15 mL) flour

1 1/4 cups (300 mL) chicken stock

freshly ground black pepper

Put cream in a saucepan and add chervil stems. Bring to a boil, then remove saucepan from heat and set aside so that cream will absorb the chervil flavor.

Melt butter in another saucepan. Add flour, stirring constantly with a whisk to make a roux. Strain the cream to remove chervil stems. Mix cream and chicken stock together, then slowly add to roux, stirring constantly until well blended. Simmer for 5 minutes. Season with pepper. Add chervil leaves, stir and serve.

Cauliflower with Chervil Mayonnaise

Crunchy cauliflower combined with the delicate taste of chervil mayonnaise makes a unique, make-ahead dish for a summer barbecue. It goes well with barbecued or baked salmon. Serves 4.

1 medium-sized cauliflower

Chervil Mayonnaise (recipe follows)

finely chopped chervil, as garnish

Break cauliflower into florets and put in a metal or Chinese bamboo steamer. Steam over boiling water for 5 minutes until tender, but still crunchy. Rinse under cold water to stop the cooking.

Put cauliflower in a bowl and add Chervil Mayonnaise. Gently mix until cauliflower is well coated. Garnish with finely-chopped chervil and chill in the refrigerator.

Chervil Mayonnaise

This delicate mayonnaise is the palest color of green and is one of summer's great pleasures. Serve with vegetables and cold fish, or use it in potato salad or coleslaw. This recipe can be made with any number of herbs: basil, chervil, chives, parsley, sorrel or tarragon, alone or in combination. Experiment with this recipe until you create a herb mayonnaise to your liking. Makes 1 1/2 cups (375 mL).

1 large egg

2 Tbsp. (30 mL) freshly squeezed lemon juice

1 Tbsp. (15 mL) Dijon mustard

1 cup (250 mL) salad or olive oil, or a combination of both

1/4 cup (50 mL) firmly packed chervil leaves

Put egg, lemon juice and mustard in a blender. Add 1/4 cup (50 mL) of the oil and blend at high speed until smooth. Add chervil and blend for a few seconds. With machine running, slowly add remaining oil and blend until mixture thickens. Chill in refrigerator until ready to use.

Cream Cheese with Chervil

For a quick, tasty hors d'oeuvre, spread this mixture on crackers or toast or stuff celery, cherry tomatoes or small lettuce leaves. This recipe can be varied using chives, tarragon, more garlic or extra pepper. Try a mixture of herbs. Makes 1 cup (250 mL).

1/2 lb. (250 g) cream cheese

1 clove garlic, peeled and crushed

1/4 cup (50 mL) chopped chervil leaves

freshly ground black pepper

Put cream cheese, garlic, chervil and pepper in a blender or food processor and process for a few seconds. You should see specks of chervil in the spread. Chill in the refrigerator for a few hours to increase the flavor.

Chervil Rice

Chervil brightens up the look and flavor of rice. If there are leftovers, serve as a rice salad with an oil and vinegar dressing. Serves 4.

3 shallots, finely chopped

3 Tbsp. (45 mL) vegetable oil

1 cup (250 mL) raw long grain white or brown rice

1/2 cup (125 mL) finely chopped chervil leaves

2 1/2 cups (625 mL) chicken stock

Sauté shallots in oil in a saucepan until limp. Add rice and stir for 2-3 minutes until straw-colored. Add chervil and chicken stock and bring to a boil. Reduce heat, cover and simmer for 20-25 minutes for white rice; 40-45 minutes for brown rice. Do not stir rice while cooking. Serve immediately.

Chervil Baking-Powder Biscuits

Serve this pretty, green-speckled biscuit with soup or salad for lunch. You can vary the herbs in this recipe. Chives, parsley, sage, dill and rosemary all work well. Makes 12 biscuits.

2 cups (500 mL) all-purpose flour

4 tsp. (20 mL) baking powder

1/4 cup (50 mL) shortening

3/4 cup (175 mL) milk

1/2 cup (125 mL) finely chopped chervil leaves

Preheat oven to 450°F (230°C). Sift flour and baking powder together. Cut in shortening with a knife or fingers and mix together until it has the consistency of cornmeal. Add milk and chervil and stir until a dough is formed.

Knead dough lightly on a floured surface a few times. Roll out and cut into biscuits. Put biscuits on an ungreased cookie sheet. Bake in preheated oven for 12-15 minutes until golden brown. To make herbed cheese biscuits, add 1/2 cup (125 mL) grated cheese to this recipe.

Chervil Butter

This herbed butter is delicious on noodles, cooked carrots, snow peas, green beans, broiled tomatoes, new potatoes or hot French bread—the possibilities are endless!

4 Tbsp. (60 mL) chopped chervil leaves

1 Tbsp. (15 mL) freshly squeezed lemon juice

1/2 cup (125 mL) softened butter

freshly ground black pepper

Put all ingredients in a blender or food processor. Process in quick spurts until mixed, and chill in a small crock. Herb butters can be frozen.

Chervil Vinegar

Follow directions for Basil Vinegar (page 12), substituting chervil. The lacy leaves look quite attractive in the bottle. The delicate flavor of Chervil Vinegar complements salads with mild-tasting lettuce. Because of its light quality, we sometimes use Japanese rice vinegar in place of white wine vinegar.

Chervil Egg Salad

Chervil makes egg salad so much more interesting. Spread on bread for an open-faced sandwich or put scoops of the salad mixture on romaine lettuce leaves for a salad plate. Serves 4.

4 hard-boiled eggs, peeled and chopped

1/4 cup (50 mL) mayonnaise

4 Tbsp. (60 mL) chopped chives

4 Tbsp. (60 mL) finely chopped chervil leaves, reserving some
     for garnish

Mix chopped eggs and mayonnaise together. Add chives and most of the chervil. Garnish with finely chopped chervil and serve.

Chervil Quiche with Ham

Use lots of chervil in this dish. The quiche tastes very good cold the next day. Serves 4-6.

1 prepared pastry shell, baked at 400°F (200°C) for 8-10 minutes

1 cup (250 mL) diced cooked ham

1 1/2 cups (375 mL) diced Swiss cheese

4 large eggs

1/2 cup (125 mL) finely chopped chervil leaves

dash of nutmeg

freshly ground black pepper

1 1/2 cups (375 mL) whipping cream

1/2 cup (125 mL) milk

Preheat oven to 325°F (160°C). Sprinkle ham and cheese on the bottom of the pastry shell. Beat eggs in a bowl. Add remaining ingredients and mix together. Pour over ham and cheese. Bake for 40 minutes until custard has set. Serve warm or cool.

Chives

*C*hives are the first of the herbs to come up in the spring. Some cooks prefer the sight of chives to the first crocus or snowdrop! Chives have a wonderful affinity with fish, cheese sauces and salads. In fact, you can add chives to any dish that has onions in it. After a winter of chopping onions and shallots, it's a treat to snip fresh green chives from your garden.

Chives are the culinary staple of your herb garden. They produce lovely mauve-pink blossoms that can be used in bouquets and salads, or to decorate platters. The blossoms also make a delicate, pale pink vinegar that is a visual delight on your kitchen shelves. Garlic chives, which come a little later in the spring, have a garlic flavor, a wider, flatter leaf and a white flower. They are used in Chinese cooking and are often seen in Chinese markets.

Growing

*C*hives are a hardy perennial. If cut frequently, they need a rich soil, fertilization every two weeks and regular watering in dry weather. Propagate by dividing a big plant into four or six divisions. Chives are easy to grow from seed, but they take longer before cutting can begin. They are a good container plant. They need a cold, dormant period in early winter. The roots quickly fill up their pots and need division and repotting at least once a year.

Chive Butter

A dollop of this butter is good on steaks, chops, broiled fish or even on hot French bread. Keep a supply on hand in the freezer.

4-5 Tbsp. (60-75 mL) chopped chives

1 Tbsp. (15 mL) freshly squeezed lemon juice

1/2 cup (125 mL) softened butter

1 anchovy fillet or a squirt of anchovy paste

freshly ground black pepper

Put all ingredients in a blender or food processor. Process until smooth and chill in a small crock. Put a dollop of the butter on each steak, chop or fish fillet just as they come off the barbecue or out of the skillet or oven.

Green Chive Dip

*As soon as the chives appear in the spring, I make this dip.
Vary the garlic, pepper and chives according to how much zip you
want in your dip. Serve with crackers or a platter of raw vegetables.*

1/2 lb. (250 g) cream cheese

1/4 cup (50 mL) yogurt

2-4 cloves garlic, peeled and crushed

1/4 cup (50 mL) chopped chives

1/4 cup (50 mL) chopped parsley

freshly ground black pepper

Put all ingredients in a blender or food processor. Process until
smooth and chill in the refrigerator for several hours to increase the
flavor. For a thinner dip, add more yogurt.

Chive Consommé

*If you have chives growing in your garden, you have the makings
of this delicious and delicate soup. You can use beef or veal stock in
place of chicken stock. Serves 4.*

4 cups (1 L) chicken stock

5 Tbsp. (75 mL) chopped chives

freshly ground black pepper

dash of dry sherry in each bowl

chopped chives, Parmesan cheese or croutons, as garnish

Warm chicken stock in a saucepan. Put chives in blender with
half the warmed stock and blend. Return blended stock to saucepan
and warm. Season with pepper. Just before serving, add a dash of
sherry to each bowl. Garnish with chopped chives, freshly grated
Parmesan cheese or homemade croutons.

Salmon Soufflé with Chives

A clever cook can impress dinner guests and use up leftover salmon with this soufflé. Serve with a green salad or fresh asparagus. Serves 4.

2 1/2 Tbsp. (40 mL) butter

3 Tbsp. (45 mL) flour

2 cups (500 mL) milk

freshly ground black pepper

2 cups (500 mL) cooked salmon, bones removed

3 eggs, separated

1/4 cup (50 mL) chopped chives

Preheat oven to 350°F (180°C). To make the sauce, melt butter in a saucepan. Add flour, stirring constantly with a whisk to make a roux. Slowly add milk to saucepan and bring to a boil, stirring constantly with a whisk until mixture thickens. Season with pepper and set aside.

Purée salmon in a blender or food processor, then transfer to a bowl. Add sauce, egg yolks and chopped chives to salmon and mix together well. Beat egg whites in a separate bowl until they are stiff. Gently fold them into fish mixture. Put mixture in a buttered soufflé dish in preheated oven for 25-30 minutes, until soufflé has risen and set and is light golden brown on top. Serve immediately.

Salmon and Chive Fish Cakes

This version of a favorite childhood dish adds a touch of horseradish and anchovy to give it piquancy. These fish cakes can be served for brunch, lunch or dinner. They go well with Chervil Sauce (page 15). They can be made with cod or other fish in place of salmon, and you can vary the herb, using chervil or tarragon instead of chives. Sometimes I replace the flour with cornmeal. Serves 4.

2 cups (500 mL) cooked salmon, bones removed

3 cups (750 mL) mashed potatoes

2 eggs, beaten

4 Tbsp. (60 mL) chopped chives

2 Tbsp. (30 mL) finely chopped parsley

1 tsp. (5 mL) horseradish

1 tsp. (5 mL) anchovy paste

freshly ground black pepper

flour

4 Tbsp. (60 mL) vegetable oil

Mix all ingredients, except flour and oil, in a large bowl. Form mixture into round cakes. Dust with flour.

Heat oil in a skillet. Fry cakes for 5 minutes per side until golden. Place on a serving platter in a warm oven until ready to serve.

Sautéed Cod with Chives, Parsley and Garlic

Sprinkling chopped herbs on the cod makes a pretty dish that will perk up your appetite. Serve it with rice and fresh green beans. Serves 4.

3 cups (750 mL) sliced mushrooms

2 cloves garlic, peeled and crushed

4 Tbsp. (60 mL) butter

4 cod steaks, approximately 1 inch (2.5 cm) thick

1/4 cup (50 mL) flour

freshly ground black pepper

4 Tbsp. (60 mL) chopped chives

4 Tbsp. (60 mL) finely chopped parsley

Sauté mushrooms and garlic in butter in a skillet for 4-5 minutes. Remove to a serving platter and keep warm in the oven.

Dredge cod steaks in flour and season with pepper. Quickly sauté cod in skillet for 3 minutes per side until golden brown. Add more butter to skillet, if necessary. Remove sautéed mushrooms and garlic from oven and add to cod in skillet. Sprinkle with chives and parsley. Cook for an additional 2-3 minutes until heated through. Serve on platter or on heated individual plates.

Jansson's Temptation
(Baked Cod with Chives and Anchovies)

They call this dish "Scandinavian downfall." There are as many versions of it as there are temptations! Serves 4.

4 Tbsp. (60 mL) butter

3-4 potatoes, peeled and sliced

1 bay leaf

3 large onions, sliced

1/4 cup (50 mL) chopped chives

1/4 cup (50 mL) finely chopped parsley

12 anchovy fillets

4 cod steaks, approximately 1 inch (2.5 cm) thick

3/4 cup (175 mL) half-and-half cream

freshly ground black pepper

Preheat oven to 375ºF (190ºC). Butter a 9 x 13 inch (23 x 34 cm) baking dish with 2 Tbsp. (30 mL) of the butter.

Layer ingredients, starting with potatoes, bay leaf, half the sliced onion, half the chopped chives and parsley, half the anchovy fillets and all of the cod. Repeat with the remaining sliced onion, chopped chives and parsley, and anchovy fillets. Pour cream over top and season with pepper. Dot with remaining 2 Tbsp. (30 mL) butter. Bake in preheated oven for 45 minutes until potatoes are tender. Serve with fresh garden peas.

Sole Marsala with Chives

The marsala and fish stock make a delicious sauce and they glaze the fish nicely. Sherry may be substituted for marsala and clam nectar for fish stock. Serve it with small new potatoes and fresh garden peas. Serves 4.

4 large fillets of sole

flour

3-4 Tbsp. (45-60 mL) butter

freshly ground black pepper

1/4 cup (50 mL) marsala

1/4 cup (50 mL) fish stock

1/4 cup (50 mL) chopped chives

Dust sole with flour. Quickly sauté sole in butter in a skillet on both sides until browned. Season with pepper. Add marsala, fish stock and chives to skillet and simmer for a few minutes until sauce has thickened and fish is cooked.

Simple Baked Sole with Chives

This is an easy oven-baked dish. Wine, clam nectar and chives team well with the mild-flavored fish. Serves 4.

4 large fillets of sole

1/4 cup (50 mL) dry white wine, or vermouth

1/4 cup (50 mL) fish stock, or clam nectar

2 Tbsp. (30 mL) freshly squeezed lemon juice

2 Tbsp. (30 mL) butter

freshly ground black pepper

3 Tbsp. (45 mL) chopped chives

Preheat oven to 350°F (180°C). Put sole in a buttered 8 x 12 inch (20 x 30 cm) baking dish. Pour wine, fish stock or clam nectar, and lemon juice over sole. Dot with butter. Season with pepper and sprinkle with chives. Bake in preheated oven for 12-15 minutes, spooning juice over sole occasionally.

Baked Halibut with Sour Cream and Chives

We all know about sour cream and chives on baked potatoes. Try it with halibut and serve a baked potato on the side! Serves 4.

4 halibut steaks, approximately 1 inch (2.5 cm) thick

freshly ground black pepper

2 Tbsp. (30 mL) butter

2 cups (500 mL) sliced mushrooms

1 cup (250 mL) sour cream

1/4 cup (50 mL) dry sherry

4 Tbsp. (60 mL) chopped chives

Preheat oven to 400°F (200°C). Put halibut in a buttered 8 x 12 inch (20 x 30 cm) baking dish. Season with pepper. Melt butter in a skillet and sauté mushrooms for 3 minutes. Add sour cream, sherry and chives to skillet and mix together. Simmer for 1 minute, then pour mixture over halibut. Bake in preheated oven for 25-30 minutes or until fish flakes.

Oyster Chowder with Chives

An excellent Sunday night supper! Serve it with crusty bread.
M.F.K. Fisher has written a delightful essay on the making of oyster
chowder in her book, The Art of Eating. *Serves 3-4.*

1 1/2 cups (375 mL) chopped onions

2 Tbsp. (30 mL) butter

2 cups (500 mL) shucked oysters, with liquid

1 cup (250 mL) cold water

2 2/3 cups (650 mL) peeled and cubed potatoes

freshly ground black pepper

1 bay leaf

4 Tbsp. (60 mL) chopped chives

3 cups (750 mL) milk

dash of hot-pepper sauce

chopped chives, as garnish

In a pot, sauté onions in butter until limp. Add oyster liquid,
water and cubed potatoes, and bring to a boil. Season with pepper.
Add bay leaf and chives. Simmer for 10-12 minutes until potatoes
are tender. Add milk and hot-pepper sauce and bring to a boil once
again.

Add oysters and remove from heat. Allow oysters to heat through
for a few minutes, then serve in heated bowls. Generously garnish
with chopped chives.

Herb Blossom Salad

This salad with mauve pink chive flowers and bright yellow and red nasturtiums is a visual delight. Chive flowers have a mild garlic taste and nasturtiums are peppery. We use chive flowers to decorate food all summer. A whole poached salmon looks most elegant surrounded by these blossoms. Borage, mint, sage, rosemary, thyme, oregano, fennel and dill also produce flowers that can be used in salads or as edible decorations. Serves 4.

2 heads butter lettuce, washed and torn into pieces

1 cup (250 mL) chive flowers

1 cup (250 mL) nasturtium flowers

3/4 cup (175 mL) vegetable oil

1/4 cup (50 mL) herbed vinegar

freshly ground black pepper

Put lettuce in a salad bowl and sprinkle chive and nasturtium flowers on top.

Mix oil, vinegar and pepper in a small jar and shake vigorously. Toss salad with just enough dressing to coat greens and serve.

Chive and Parsley Omelette

If you are dining alone, this recipe is for you. The herbs brighten up the standard omelette. You can use basil, chervil, fennel, sorrel, tarragon or a mixture in place of the chives and parsley. Serves 1.

3 large eggs

3 Tbsp. (45 mL) cold water

freshly ground black pepper

1/4 cup (50 mL) chopped chives

1/4 cup (50 mL) finely chopped parsley

1 Tbsp. (15 mL) butter

Beat eggs in a bowl. Add water, pepper, chives and parsley and mix together well. Melt butter in an 8-inch (20-cm) skillet over medium-high heat, letting it get brown and bubbly. Pour eggs into skillet and slide them back and forth to avoid sticking. When bottom is set, tip pan so that eggs run into the middle. When eggs are no longer runny, fold omelette over and slide onto a warm plate. The omelette should be moist inside.

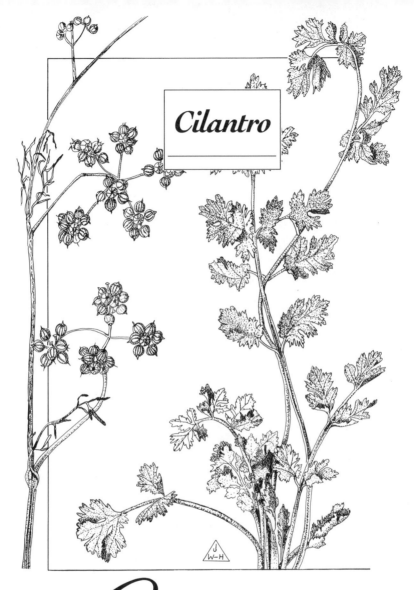

Cilantro

*C*ilantro is used by many cuisines. Those who have travelled to Mexico, California or India often come home with a taste for this pungent, unusual herb. Cilantro grows easily and is usually available in most Chinese markets. It is excellent in stir-fries and salads. The seeds of the plant are known as coriander seeds and are used in baking. Cilantro has a strong, musky, licorice flavor that grows on you!

Growing

C ilantro is an annual herb that is also called coriander, Chinese parsley or Mexican parsley. Soak seeds for 24 hours before sowing in late spring, or earlier, under plastic. Cilantro needs a fairly rich soil and frequent watering during dry spells. It is suitable for large containers.

Zucchini and Cilantro Stir-Fry

Many different vegetables can be substituted for the zucchini; try broccoli, snow peas, green beans, onions or celery. You can add chopped chicken, pork, beef or shrimp to this dish—a good way to use leftover meat. Serves 4.

2-3 Tbsp. (30-45 mL) vegetable oil

4 cups (1 L) thinly sliced zucchini

1 cup (250 mL) chopped onions or chopped green onions

1/2 cup (125 mL) chicken stock

2 Tbsp. (30 mL) cornstarch

3-4 Tbsp. (45-60 mL) cold water

1/4 cup (50 mL) finely chopped cilantro

dash of soy sauce

Heat oil in a wok or skillet. Quickly stir-fry zucchini and onions until vegetables are coated with oil. Add chicken stock, cover, and simmer for 2-3 minutes.

Mix cornstarch and water together. Add cornstarch mixture and cilantro to wok or skillet and stir until sauce thickens. Add a dash of soy sauce and serve.

Cilantro Pepper Cream Cheese

A combination of fresh cilantro and dried coriander seeds makes a pungent, peppery spread. It is interesting to use both parts of the plant. I spread this on bagels for Sunday brunch. Serves 8-10.

1/2 lb. (250 g) cream cheese

1/4 cup (50 mL) chopped cilantro

3 Tbsp. (45 mL) coriander seeds, partially cracked with
   a mortar and pestle

2 Tbsp. (30 mL) freshly ground black pepper

Put all ingredients in a food processor. Process until just mixed. Serve in a bowl decorated with cilantro leaves along the edges and a few coriander seeds sprinkled on top.

Cilantro Raita

This cool mixture calms the palate, so serve it with curries, barbecued meats and other spicy dishes. It is a good sauce for rice, vegetables or baked potatoes. Makes 2 1/2 cups (625 mL).

2 cups (500 mL) yogurt

1 medium cucumber, peeled and grated

2 green onions, finely chopped

2 cloves garlic, peeled and chopped

1/2 cup (125 mL) finely chopped cilantro

freshly ground black pepper

Mix ingredients together in a bowl and chill in refrigerator for a few hours before serving.

Cauliflower and Cilantro Salad

This is an interesting change from lettuce salads. It looks good on an antipasto plate with other marinated vegetables. Serves 6.

1 medium-sized cauliflower

1/4 cup (50 mL) finely chopped cilantro

3/4 cup (175 mL) vegetable oil

1/4 cup (50 mL) herbed vinegar

freshly ground black pepper

Break cauliflower into florets and put in a metal or Chinese bamboo steamer. Steam over boiling water for 5 minutes until tender, but still crunchy. Rinse under cold water to stop the cooking. Put cauliflower in a bowl and add cilantro. Mix oil, vinegar and pepper together. Pour dressing over cauliflower and chill in refrigerator until ready to serve. Marinated cauliflower will keep in the refrigerator for several days.

Cilantro Mayonnaise

This can be made the cheater's way by using good-quality, store-bought mayonnaise and adding 1/4 cup (50 mL) chopped cilantro to 1 cup (250 mL) mayonnaise, or you can quickly make your own blender mayonnaise and add cilantro. See the recipe for Chervil Mayonnaise (page 16) and substitute 1/4 cup (50 mL) firmly packed cilantro leaves for the chervil leaves. Cilantro Mayonnaise tastes very good on cold shrimp, crab, salmon eggs or tomatoes.

Indian Apple Chutney
with Cilantro and Coriander

This chutney is delicious with cold meats, curries, cheese, sausage or barbecued hamburgers. Instead of apples, you can use peaches or pears. Makes 8 cups (2 L).

12 tart green apples, peeled, cored and diced

8 medium onions, chopped

6 large cloves garlic, peeled and chopped

3 1/2 cups (875 mL) red wine vinegar

2 1/2 cups (625 mL) brown sugar

1 Tbsp. (15 mL) cracked coriander seeds

6 whole black peppercorns

6 whole allspice

6 Tbsp. (90 mL) chopped candied ginger

1 Tbsp. (15 mL) salt

1/2 cup (125 mL) chopped cilantro

Put apples, onions and garlic in a pot. Add vinegar and sugar and bring to a boil. Reduce heat to low and simmer for 30 minutes until apples are tender, but not mushy.

Add coriander seeds, whole peppercorns, whole allspice, chopped candied ginger and salt and simmer for 1 hour, or until mixture is thick. When mixture is thick, add cilantro and stir. Put chutney in sterilized jars and seal. Store in a cool, dark place for several weeks to improve the flavor.

Zucchini Soup with Cilantro

Mild-tasting, overabundant zucchini needs a flavor boost and pungent cilantro does the job in this soup. Serves 6.

2 medium onions, sliced

3 Tbsp. (45 mL) vegetable oil

4 cups (1 L) puréed zucchini, skin on (choose tender young ones)

4 cups (1 L) chicken stock

1/4 cup (50 mL) finely chopped cilantro

freshly ground black pepper

yogurt and finely chopped cilantro, as garnish

In a skillet, sauté onions in oil over medium heat for 2-3 minutes. Add to puréed zucchini in blender or food processor and process until smooth.

Combine puréed vegetables, chicken stock, cilantro and pepper in a pot and simmer over low heat for 10 minutes. Serve in heated bowls with a dollop of yogurt on top. Garnish with finely chopped cilantro. To serve cold, chill in refrigerator for several hours. Serve with several ice cubes floating in the soup.

Tomato Salad with Cilantro

So simple and so good, this is a variation of Tomato and Basil Salad. Serves 4.

4 ripe tomatoes, sliced

3/4 cup (175 mL) vegetable oil

1/4 cup (50 mL) freshly squeezed lemon juice

freshly ground black pepper

1/4 cup (50 mL) finely chopped cilantro

Lay tomato slices on a platter. Mix oil, lemon juice and pepper together in a bowl. Sprinkle chopped cilantro over tomato slices. Pour oil and lemon juice dressing over top. You will not need all the dressing but it keeps well in the refrigerator. Use it as a basic vinaigrette with other vegetable and herb combinations.

Shrimp with Tequila and Cilantro

Serve this creamy shrimp with tequila over rice or noodles. Serves 2.

1 lb. (500 g) raw large peeled shrimp

1/4 cup (50 mL) freshly squeezed lime juice (reserve some for the avocado)

freshly ground black pepper

2 Tbsp. (30 mL) chopped shallots

3 Tbsp. (45 mL) butter

1/4 cup (50 mL) whipping cream

1/4 cup (50 mL) tequila

1 avocado, peeled, sliced and sprinkled with freshly squeezed lime juice

1/4 cup (50 mL) chopped cilantro

Put peeled shrimp in a bowl and sprinkle with lime juice. Marinate for 15 minutes. Season with pepper. Sauté drained shrimp and shallots in butter in a skillet for 2 minutes. Add cream and tequila and bring to a boil, then reduce heat to low and simmer for 2 minutes. Add sliced avocado and heat through. Stir in chopped cilantro. Olé!

Dill

To use dill just for pickle-making in the late summer is to ignore its wonderful flavor in soups, salads, fish dishes and in baking. The fine leaves, as well as the young flower heads, can be used in cooking.

Growing

*D*ill is an annual. Sow outside each month in early through late spring for successive crops. Dill does best in fairly rich soil. It can be grown in large containers and can be cut when it is about 12 inches (30 cm) high, though most dill is cut when plants reach 3 feet (1 m) and form seed heads. Dill will self-sow the second year after planting, sometimes in unexpected places!

Dilled Grilled Salmon Steaks

Grilled salmon steaks combined with the first new potatoes from the garden or market—this is my idea of culinary bliss. Serves 4.

4 salmon steaks, approximately 1 inch (2.5 cm) thick

1/4 cup (50 mL) vegetable oil

juice of 1 lemon

4 Tbsp. (60 mL) finely chopped dill

freshly ground black pepper

4 Tbsp. (60 mL) butter, melted

lemon slices and dill fronds, as garnish

Put salmon steaks in a baking dish. Mix oil, lemon juice, dill and pepper together and pour over salmon. Cover baking dish with plastic wrap and chill in refrigerator for 1 hour, turning salmon 2-3 times.

Preheat oven to broil/grill. Broil/grill salmon steaks on a rack, 3 inches (7.5 cm) from element, for 4-5 minutes per side. Put salmon steaks on hot plates. Pour melted butter over steaks and garnish with dill fronds and lemon slices. Serve at once.

Salmon Quiche with Dill and Parsley

The pink salmon, yellow eggs and green herbs make this an attractive dish for a luncheon. You can use shrimp, crab or any other kind of fish in place of salmon. Serves 4-6.

1 prepared pastry shell, baked at 400°F (200°C) for 8-10 minutes

1 cup (250 mL) cooked, flaked salmon, bones removed

4 Tbsp. (60 mL) finely chopped dill

2 Tbsp. (30 mL) finely chopped parsley

4 large eggs

1/4 cup (50 mL) half-and-half cream

1/4 cup (50 mL) freshly grated Parmesan cheese

freshly ground black pepper

Preheat oven to 350°F (180°F). Sprinkle salmon on the bottom of the pastry shell. Sprinkle dill and parsley on top of salmon.

Beat eggs in a bowl. Add cream and Parmesan cheese to eggs and mix together. Season with pepper and pour over salmon and herbs in pastry shell. Bake in preheated oven for 40 minutes until custard has set. Serve warm or cool.

Cucumber Dill Summer Soup

The combination of cucumber, yogurt and dill is very soothing on a hot summer day. Chill glass serving bowls in the freezer for a few minutes before serving. Serves 2-3.

1 large cucumber, skin on, grated

2 cups (500 mL) yogurt

1 clove garlic, peeled and crushed

2 Tbsp. (30 mL) white wine vinegar

1/4 cup (50 mL) finely chopped dill, reserving some for garnish

freshly ground black pepper

Mix ingredients together in a bowl and chill in refrigerator until ready to serve. Before serving, garnish with finely chopped dill.

Smoked Salmon Pâté with Dill

Clever cooks learn many variations for the same ingredients. This salmon pâté has a different flavor because the salmon is smoked and cream cheese is substituted for butter. Serves 4-6.

6 oz. (175 g) smoked salmon

1/2 lb. (250 g) cream cheese

2 Tbsp. (30 mL) finely chopped shallots

3 Tbsp. (45 mL) freshly squeezed lemon juice

3 Tbsp. (45 mL) chopped dill

freshly ground black pepper

finely chopped dill, as garnish

Put all ingredients except garnish in a food processor. Process until smooth and chill in a small crock. Before serving, garnish with finely chopped dill on top. This recipe can be thinned with the addition of a little mayonnaise and used as a dip with crackers or chips.

Gravlax with Dill

The marinated salmon tastes just like smoked salmon, which is more expensive to buy. You can use fennel in place of dill. Serve with thin slices of rye bread or with crackers. Serves 8-12 as an hors d'oeuvre.

1/4 cup (50 mL) chopped dill

2-lb. (1-kg) fresh fillet of salmon, boned, with the skin left on

3 Tbsp. (45 mL) kosher pickling salt

4 Tbsp. (60 mL) sugar

1/2 tsp. (2 mL) freshly ground black pepper

1/2 tsp. (2 mL) ground allspice

1/4 cup (50 mL) vinegar

Put half the chopped dill in the bottom of a baking pan. Place salmon fillet, skin side down, on top of dill.

Mix salt, sugar, pepper and allspice together in a bowl. Pat salmon with spice mixture. Pour vinegar over salmon and sprinkle with the remaining dill.

Cover baking dish with plastic wrap and chill in refrigerator with a brick on top of wrap for at least 24 hours. Spoon brine juices over salmon occasionally. To serve, wipe salmon clean and place on a wooden board, skin side down. Slice very thinly at an angle.

Dilled New Potatoes

This method of herbing vegetables can be used for carrots, peas, zucchini, beans and many other vegetables. In place of dill, you can use parsley, summer savory or tarragon.

Boil or steam new potatoes until they are tender. Melt 2 Tbsp. (30 mL) butter in a saucepan and add 3 Tbsp. (45 mL) finely chopped dill. Coat potatoes in butter and dill, then serve.

Dill Poached Sole

The sauce in this dish is made from the poaching milk, and it is delicious. Serve it with rice, noodles or small new potatoes. Serves 4.

2 cups (500 mL) milk

6 whole allspice

freshly ground black pepper

1 bay leaf

4 large fillets of sole

1 medium onion, thinly sliced

4 Tbsp. (60 mL) butter

3 Tbsp. (45 mL) flour

3 Tbsp. (45 mL) dry sherry

4 Tbsp. (60 mL) finely chopped dill

finely chopped dill, as garnish

Combine milk, allspice, pepper and bay leaf in a skillet and heat until it begins to bubble. Add sole and cover with onion. Poach sole over medium heat for 5 minutes, until fish flakes. Remove from skillet to a serving platter; keep warm in the oven.

Pour poaching liquid through a fine sieve into a bowl. Melt butter in a saucepan. Add flour, stirring constantly with a whisk to make a roux. Slowly add poaching liquid to roux, stirring constantly until well blended. Add sherry and dill and simmer for 5 minutes until sauce thickens. Pour sauce over sole and garnish with finely chopped dill.

Dilled Tuna Fish or Egg Salad Sandwiches

Make a regular tuna fish or egg salad sandwich and add 1/4 cup (50 mL) finely chopped dill. Dill gives these usually mundane lunch standbys a sharp, new taste. You can use chervil, fennel or tarragon in place of dill.

Tomato Dill Soup

When you have a glut of ripe tomatoes, this recipe provides a solution. This adaptable soup can be served hot or cold and it freezes well. Serves 4.

1 cup (250 mL) chopped onions

several sprigs of parsley

3 Tbsp. (45 mL) vegetable oil

12 ripe tomatoes, peeled and coarsely chopped

3 cups (750 mL) chicken stock

1/4 cup (50 mL) chopped dill

freshly ground black pepper

finely chopped dill and yogurt or sour cream, as garnish

Sauté onions and parsley in oil in a pot for 3 minutes. Add tomatoes, chicken stock and dill to pot and bring to a boil. Season with pepper. Reduce heat to low and simmer for 15 minutes.

Purée soup in a blender or food processor. Serve hot or cold. Garnish with dill and a dollop of yogurt or sour cream.

Dill Yogurt Dressing

Serve this as a dip with fresh raw vegetables or use it on baked potatoes or salads. Makes 2 cups (500 mL).

1 1/2 cups (375 mL) yogurt

1/2 cup (125 mL) mayonnaise

1 clove garlic, peeled and crushed

2 Tbsp. (30 mL) freshly squeezed lemon juice

1/2 cup (125 mL) finely chopped dill

freshly ground black pepper

Mix all ingredients together and chill in refrigerator until ready to use.

Shrimp with Beer and Lemon-Dill Butter

Your guests do all the work with this hors d'oeuvre. You might want to have finger bowls and hot towels handy! Serves 4-6.

1 1/2 lbs. (700 g) raw unpeeled shrimp

1 (10 fl. oz./355 mL) bottle beer

2 cloves garlic, peeled and crushed

4 Tbsp. (60 mL) finely chopped dill

1 bay leaf

several sprigs of parsley

dash of hot-pepper sauce

dash of allspice

Lemon-Dill Butter (recipe follows)

Put all ingredients in a pot and bring to a boil. Reduce heat to low and simmer for 2 minutes, then strain. Put shrimp in a large bowl. Let your guests peel their own shrimp. Serve with Lemon-Dill Butter.

Lemon-Dill Butter

1/2 cup (125 mL) butter

3 Tbsp. (45 mL) freshly squeezed lemon juice

2 Tbsp. (30 mL) finely chopped dill

freshly ground black pepper

Melt butter in a saucepan. Add lemon juice and dill and mix together. Serve in small bowls for dipping.

Cucumber-Dill Seafood Sauce

Versatile, cool and smooth, this sauce can be used on cold fish, crab, shrimp or fresh raw vegetables. Makes about 3 cups (750 mL).

2 cups (500 mL) peeled, seeded and chopped cucumber

1 cup (250 mL) sour cream

1 cup (250 mL) mayonnaise

juice of 1 lemon

1/4 cup (50 mL) finely chopped dill

freshly ground black pepper

Mix ingredients together in a bowl and chill in refrigerator until ready to serve.

Sautéed Cucumber with Dill

Cooked cucumber is an elegant and surprising dish that is particularly compatible with fish. Cucumbers can be sautéed, braised, steamed or baked. As you will see, dill goes well with both pickled and unpickled cucumbers. Serves 4.

2 medium cucumbers, peeled, seeded and chopped

2 Tbsp. (30 mL) butter or vegetable oil

4 Tbsp. (60 mL) finely chopped dill

freshly ground black pepper

Sauté cucumber in butter or oil for 2-3 minutes. Add dill, season with pepper and serve.

Fennel

*H*erb fennel, with its feathery leaves and seed heads, looks like dill, but it has an anise licorice flavor that is quite unique. Both herb and vegetable fennel are a favorite in Italian cuisine. They are used in many fish dishes and for barbecuing and roasting meats, especially pork. Fennel is also good in soups, salads, cheese and egg dishes. It makes a wonderful addition to cream cheese sandwiches with a slice of tomato.

Fennel is very beautiful in the garden. We use it in summer bouquets and as an edible garnish.

Growing

There are two fennels, the herb and the vegetable. The herb fennel (*foeniculum vulgare*) is a perennial and should be sown in early spring in ordinary garden soil. Old plants can be divided in late winter and replanted. Herb fennel grows close to 5 feet (1.5 m) high and looks good at the back of a flower bed. It is not very frost-hardy—in northern areas it should be grown as an annual. It can also be grown in containers, and can be overwintered in large containers in a cool greenhouse.

Vegetable fennel, known as Florentine or sweet fennel, is an annual vegetable. We plant it in early summer. It is a good fall, cold-weather vegetable. It has a huge bulbous base and its leaf fronds taste and look similar to the herb fennel. The base is used raw or cooked; the fronds are used as a herb, as their flavor is identical.

Barbecued Cod with Fennel

An adaptation of a famous Mediterranean dish, the scent of the fennel sprigs on the barbecue is tantalizing. You can use red snapper in place of cod. Serves 4.

1 whole cod, about 3 lbs. (1.5 kg), cleaned, without the head

freshly ground black pepper

4 Tbsp. (60 mL) olive oil

2 cups (500 mL) fennel sprigs and stalks

4 Tbsp. (60 mL) finely chopped fennel

4 Tbsp. (60 mL) butter, melted

Prepare barbecue. Season cod inside and out with pepper. Brush inside and out with oil. Put a few fennel sprigs inside fish. Lay remaining fennel sprigs and fennel stalks on coals of barbecue.

Oil grill. Put cod on barbecue, 5-6 inches (12.5-15 cm) from hot coals, and cook for 8 minutes per side until fish is done. Put cod on a serving platter, and peel skin off and discard. Add chopped fennel to melted butter, pour over cod and serve.

Baked Cod with Fennel Stuffing

Vegetable fennel tastes like licorice-flavored celery. Vermouth is a white wine steeped in herbs, and improves sauces. Serves 4.

2 bulbs fennel, sliced, reserving 3 Tbsp. (45 mL) fennel
   leaves for garnish

1 large onion, finely chopped

3 cloves garlic, peeled and crushed

4 Tbsp. (60 mL) butter

4 fillets of cod

freshly ground black pepper

1 cup (250 mL) dry vermouth

3 Tbsp. (45 mL) butter

Preheat oven to 350°F (180°C). Boil fennel in a pot of water for 5 minutes, then drain. Sauté fennel, onion and garlic in 4 Tbsp. (60 mL) butter for 5 minutes. Place in a buttered casserole dish and put cod on top of vegetables. Season with pepper. Pour vermouth over cod, and dot with 3 Tbsp. (45 mL) butter.

Bake casserole in preheated oven for 20 minutes. Serve on a bed of rice with vegetables on top of cod. Use the pan juices as the sauce. Garnish with reserved finely chopped fennel leaves.

Fennel Cheese Sauce for Pasta

This smooth cheese sauce has just a hint of fennel. Use the herb fennel. For an extra touch, you could add shrimp or mushrooms to the sauce. Serves 4.

3 Tbsp. (45 mL) butter

3 Tbsp. (45 mL) flour

2 cups (500 mL) milk

1/2 cup (125 mL) freshly grated Swiss cheese

1/2 cup (125 mL) freshly grated Parmesan cheese

1/2 cup (125 mL) finely chopped fennel

1 lb. (500 g) cooked pasta

Parmesan cheese, as garnish

Melt butter in a saucepan. Add flour, stirring constantly with a whisk to make a roux. Slowly add milk to saucepan and bring to a boil, stirring constantly with a whisk until mixture thickens. Add Swiss cheese and Parmesan cheese to saucepan and stir until well blended. Add fennel and mix together. Toss well with the hot, cooked pasta, and serve immediately. At the table, sprinkle with extra freshly grated Parmesan cheese.

Fennel Cream Soup

This elegant soup makes a fine beginning for a summer dinner party. Use the herb fennel. Serves 4.

1 cup (250 mL) finely chopped celery

1 medium onion, finely chopped

4 Tbsp. (60 mL) butter

2 Tbsp. (30 mL) flour

3 cups (750 mL) chicken stock

3/4 cup (175 mL) half-and-half cream

1/2 cup (125 mL) finely chopped fennel

finely chopped fennel, as garnish

Sauté celery and onion in butter for 5 minutes. Sprinkle with flour and continue to cook for 3-4 minutes. Slowly add chicken stock to saucepan and bring to a boil. Reduce heat to low and simmer for 15 minutes.

While chicken stock is simmering, heat cream in another saucepan and add fennel. Remove from heat and let sit until chicken stock has finished simmering. This will increase the fennel flavor in the cream. Slowly whisk cream into chicken stock. Heat through and serve. Garnish with finely chopped fennel.

Roast Pork with Fennel

An Italian chef we know cooks suckling pig stuffed with fennel leaves and branches. Pork and fennel make good culinary companions. Try a little finely chopped fennel on pork chops, ground pork meatballs or pork meat loaf. Use the herb fennel. Serves 4-6.

6 Tbsp. (90 mL) softened butter

4 Tbsp. (60 mL) finely chopped fennel

freshly ground black pepper

1 4-lb. (2-kg) roast of pork

Preheat oven to 325°F (160°C). Mix butter and fennel together. Season with pepper. Spread thinly over roast pork. Use all the mixture.

Put pork in a roasting pan and roast for 2 1/2–3 hours. Use a meat thermometer. When roast is ready it should read 170°F (75°C). Roast potatoes in the pan with the pork, and make a gravy with the herb-flavored drippings.

Baked Sole
with Mussels and Fennelled Cream Sauce

A creamy fish dish—fit for company. Serves 4.

4 large fillets of sole

freshly ground black pepper

3 cups (750 mL) sliced mushrooms

1/2 cup (125 mL) dry white wine

18 fresh mussels, washed and scrubbed

1/2 cup (125 mL) cold water

3 Tbsp. (45 mL) butter

4 Tbsp. (60 mL) flour

1 1/2 cups (375 mL) milk

4 Tbsp. (60 mL) finely chopped fennel

Preheat oven to 375ºF (190ºC). Place sole in buttered casserole dish and season with pepper. Put sliced mushrooms on top of sole and pour wine over mushrooms and sole. Bake for 10-12 minutes.

While sole is baking, steam mussels in a pot with water for 5-6 minutes until the shells open. Remove mussels from shells and set aside. Melt butter in a saucepan. Add flour, stirring constantly with a whisk to make a roux. Slowly add milk and bring to a boil, stirring constantly with a whisk until mixture thickens. Add the chopped fennel.

Remove casserole dish from oven and increase heat to broil/grill. Sole should only be partially cooked at this point. Arrange mussels around the sole, and pour the sauce over top. Return casserole dish to oven and broil/grill for 2 minutes until sauce is bubbling and golden.

Horseradish

*H*orseradish is a decided asset in your herb garden. It contains vitamins and minerals and it makes a good salt substitute. We dig the root when we need it, for it has no season. Peel and chop horseradish, then put it in your blender or food processor with some vinegar to moisten and you have your own fresh horseradish which will keep in the refrigerator for months. The new small leaves of the plant in the springtime add a sprightly taste to salads.

Growing

*H*orseradish ia a hardy perennial. It is easy to grow and hard to get rid of! One plant is probably enough for a small family. Only a small piece of the root is necessary to make a new plant. Root sections from established plants can be removed at any time of the year. In cold climates, the roots should be dug before the ground freezes, keeping a portion in damp sand in the basement for early planting in the spring in fairly rich soil. Horseradish is only suitable for large containers.

Horseradish, Beet and Sour Cream Sauce

Color affects the appetite, and the lovely pink shade of this sauce, along with its piquant taste, perks up beef, hot or cold. It is a dynamite ingredient in a cold meat sandwich. Makes 2 cups (500 mL).

- 1 cup (250 mL) sour cream
- 1 cup (250 mL) diced cooked beets
- 4 Tbsp. (60 mL) grated fresh horseradish, or 4 Tbsp. (60 mL) horseradish-vinegar mixture

Put ingredients in a blender or food processor. Process until smooth and chill in refrigerator until ready to serve.

Horseradish Seafood Sauce

A favorite summertime lunch at the farm is a huge platter of cracked crab, French bread, melted butter with lemon, and this seafood sauce. Makes 1 cup (250 mL).

1/2 cup (125 mL) chili sauce

1/2 cup (125 mL) mayonnaise

2 Tbsp. (30 mL) grated fresh horseradish, or 2 Tbsp. (30 mL) horseradish-vinegar mixture

dash of hot-pepper sauce

freshly ground black pepper

Mix ingredients together in a bowl and serve in small bowls with seafood.

Horseradish Mayonnaise

Add 2 Tbsp. (30 mL) grated fresh horseradish to 1 cup (250 mL) homemade or store-bought mayonnaise. Serve with cold roast beef or ham.

Horseradish Bloody Mary

Omit the hot-pepper sauce in your Bloody Mary and add 1 tsp. (5 mL) grated fresh horseradish instead. This makes a good wake-up drink for Sunday brunch!

Horseradish Mustard

This is for those who like their condiments hot!

1/4 cup (50 mL) dry mustard

enough white wine vinegar to make a smooth paste

2 Tbsp. (30 mL) grated fresh horseradish

1 tsp. (5 mL) freshly grated black pepper

Mix ingredients together in a bowl and store in the refrigerator. If you want a milder horseradish mustard, add the horseradish to Dijon mustard.

Horseradish Sauce for Vegetables

Creamy smooth, with a devilish bit of horseradish, this sauce is great on tomatoes, cucumbers, asparagus, or any cold salad vegetable. Makes 1 cup (250 mL).

1 cup (250 mL) whipping cream, whipped, or 1 cup (250 mL) yogurt, or 1 cup (250 mL) sour cream

juice of 1 lemon

2-3 Tbsp. (30-45 mL) grated fresh horseradish

1 Tbsp. (15 mL) sugar

freshly ground black pepper

Mix ingredients together in a bowl and chill in refrigerator until ready to serve.

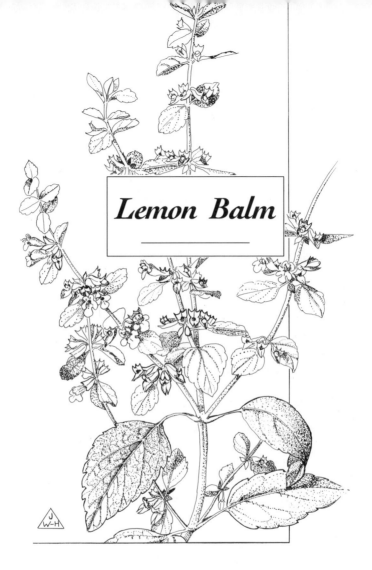

Lemon Balm

*L*emon balm is a neglected herb. It is a delight to have in your garden. Pick a leaf, scrunch it and smell it! Lemon balm has many culinary possibilities. It belongs to the mint family and can be used in many of the same ways but, in addition, you get a lemon tang from it.

Growing

A hardy perennial, lemon balm may be grown from seed, cuttings or division of the whole plant. Lemon balm needs some shade and can tolerate temperatures to 20°F (–7°C). You can grow lemon balm in your flower bed or in containers.

Lemon Balm Tea (Hot or Cold)

This tea is said to alleviate depression and lift the spirits. Serves 3-4.

1 tea bag Earl Grey tea

1 handful lemon balm leaves, reserving a few for garnish

several slices of lemon

Put ingredients in a large teapot and pour boiling water over them. Allow tea to steep for 5 minutes. Serve with a fresh lemon balm leaf in each cup. Sweeten with honey. This tea looks beautiful in Russian glass teacups.

To serve cold, let tea steep for 8-10 minutes. Strain into a jug and chill in refrigerator until ready to serve. Serve over ice in a glass, with a slice of lemon and a fresh lemon balm leaf in each glass. Sweeten with honey.

Lemon Balm White Wine Cup

Serve this cooling lemon-scented drink before dinner on a warm summer evening. Serves 4.

1 cup (250 mL) lemon balm leaves

4 cups (1 L) chilled white Chablis wine

Put lemon balm and 1 tray of ice cubes in a large glass jug. Pour wine into jug and stir. Serve in chilled wine glasses, with a fresh lemon balm leaf in each glass.

Roast Lamb with Lemon Balm

This lamb is especially moist and flavorful. Serve it with Lemon Balm Jelly (page 63). The roast can also be cooked on the barbecue. Serves 6.

1 4-lb. (2-kg) roast of lamb, leg or shoulder

freshly ground black pepper

2 cups (500 mL) lemon balm leaves

Preheat oven to 325°F (160°C). Put lamb on a large piece of aluminum foil on the rack of a roasting pan. There should be enough aluminum foil to wrap the roast. Season lamb with pepper, then arrange lemon balm on top. Tightly wrap lamb with foil.

Roast for 45 minutes. Remove pan from oven and remove aluminum foil. Remove lemon balm and discard. Insert meat thermometer in roast, return to oven and roast for an additional 1 1/4 hours until roast is browned. Thermometer should read 140°F (60°C) for rare meat; 160°F (70°C) for medium meat; and 170-180°F (75-80°C) for well-done meat. If roast is not browned enough when it is done, increase heat in oven to broil/grill and return roasting pan to oven for a few minutes until brown. Make a gravy with the herb-flavored drippings.

Lemon Balm Butter

Use this herbed butter on barbecued, sautéed or steamed fish such as salmon, cod or halibut. Lemon balm leaves make a great decoration for a fish platter—a refreshing change from parsley.

4 Tbsp. (60 mL) chopped lemon balm

1 Tbsp. (15 mL) freshly squeezed lemon juice

1/2 cup (125 mL) softened butter

freshly ground black pepper

Put all ingredients in a blender or food processor. Process until smooth. Chill in a small crock until you need it.

Butter Lettuce and Lemon Balm Salad

This delicately lemon-flavored salad tastes of spring. Serves 2.

1 head butter lettuce, washed, torn and dried

1/4 cup (50 mL) chopped lemon balm leaves

3/4 cup (175 mL) light vegetable oil

1/4 cup (50 mL) freshly squeezed lemon juice

freshly ground black pepper

1 finely chopped hard-boiled egg

Mix lettuce and lemon balm leaves together in a salad bowl.

Mix oil, lemon juice and pepper together in a bottle or jar and shake vigorously. Moisten lettuce and lemon balm with dressing. You will have some left over, which can be refrigerated for later use. Sprinkle salad with finely chopped hard-boiled egg and serve.

Lemon Balm Spring Soup

Travellers to Greece will recognize this soup. You can make it with mint or tarragon in place of lemon balm. Serves 4.

4 cups (1 L) chicken stock

1/4 cup (50 mL) long grain rice

3 eggs

4 Tbsp. (60 mL) freshly squeezed lemon juice

3 Tbsp. (45 mL) finely chopped lemon balm

freshly ground black pepper

Combine chicken stock and rice in a pot and bring to a boil. Reduce heat to low, cover and simmer for 20 minutes until rice is cooked.

Beat eggs in a bowl; add lemon juice and mix together. When rice is cooked, add 1 cup (250 mL) chicken stock to egg-lemon mixture and mix together well. Return this combination to remaining chicken stock in pot, whisking the whole time. The soup should thicken slightly. Do not curdle soup by boiling it. Add lemon balm to pot. Season with pepper. Serve hot.

Lemon Balm Jelly

This recipe can be made with herbs other than lemon balm. Try mint, rosemary, sage, tarragon, thyme or a combination—all these herb jellies are delicious. We make them in late summer and store them for Christmas gifts. Herb brews tend to be a drab brown color. For rosemary jelly, we add a few drops of red food coloring; for sage and thyme, we add yellow food coloring. Herb jellies are great with roasts, chops, ham or chicken. Makes 4 small jars.

6 Tbsp. (90 mL) finely chopped lemon balm

1 1/4 cups (300 mL) boiling water

1/4 cup (50 mL) white wine vinegar

3 cups (750 mL) sugar

3 drops green food coloring

1/2 bottle (5 1/2 fl. oz./170 mL) liquid pectin

Put lemon balm and boiling water in a saucepan and allow to steep for 15 minutes.

Take 1 cup (250 mL) lemon balm liquid and put it in another saucepan. Add vinegar and sugar and bring to a boil. Add food coloring and pectin, stirring constantly. Remove saucepan from heat. Skim mixture and pour into hot, sterile jars. Seal and store.

You may want to leave some of the finely chopped lemon balm in the jelly or you may want to strain it out. We often leave the lemon balm in, as it looks attractive and improves the flavor.

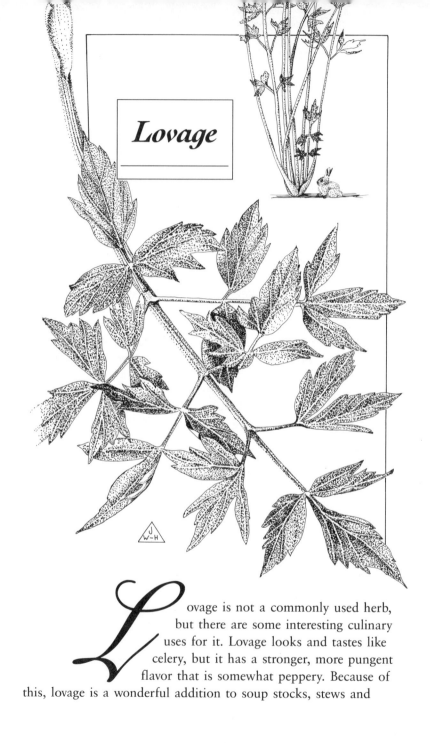

Lovage

*L*ovage is not a commonly used herb, but there are some interesting culinary uses for it. Lovage looks and tastes like celery, but it has a stronger, more pungent flavor that is somewhat peppery. Because of this, lovage is a wonderful addition to soup stocks, stews and casseroles. Try adding it to a recipe for Osso Buco or French Onion Soup. In the early spring, chop a few new leaves and put them in a salad—it gives mild lettuce an added zing. One of our restaurant clients adds it to Minestrone Soup. Lovage can be used as a celery substitute in many dishes and it can be added to breads, cheese dishes or sausage rolls for flavor. The seeds can also be used in breads, sauces, soups or stews.

Growing

A hardy perennial, lovage may be grown from seed or division of large plants in the early spring. It grows from 4 to 6 feet (1.2-2 m) in height and has attractive foliage. Lovage needs average garden soil and some shade. Seedlings and young plants are suited to containers.

Lovage Vinegar

This herb vinegar has a strong, robust flavor and is excellent for marinades, or in a dressing for coleslaw. Use the same method of preparation as used for Basil Vinegar (page 12), substituting lovage for basil.

Lovage Omelette or Scrambled Eggs

Add 2-3 Tbsp. (30-45 mL) finely chopped lovage to your favorite omelette recipe. Add the lovage in the center of the omelette just as you are about to fold it over. For scrambled eggs, add 1 Tbsp. (15 mL) finely chopped lovage to the eggs just before you beat them.

Lovage Vegetable Soup

Lovage is a useful herb for making meatless stock because it has a full, rich flavor. You can vary the vegetables in this soup, depending on what is available in your garden or at the market. Serve it with freshly grated Parmesan cheese and a loaf of crusty bread. Serves 4.

6 cups (1.5 L) cold water

1 cup (250 mL) chopped lovage leaves and stalks

1 medium onion, chopped

4 carrots, peeled and diced

1 bunch parsley, chopped

2-4 tomatoes, peeled and chopped

1 1/2 cups (375 mL) chopped green beans, cut in
    1 inch (2.5 cm) pieces

2-3 small zucchini, diced

1/2 cup (125 mL) macaroni pieces

freshly ground black pepper

Put water in a saucepan and bring to a boil. Reduce heat to low, add lovage and simmer for 15 minutes. Add onion, carrots, parsley, tomatoes, green beans and zucchini and bring to a boil once again. Reduce heat to low and simmer for 20 minutes until vegetables are soft. Add macaroni and simmer for an additional 5-8 minutes until macaroni is soft. Season with pepper.

Lovage Cheese Soufflé

A favorite herb in Germany, lovage adds a celery flavor to this cheese soufflé. Serves 4-6.

3 Tbsp. (45 mL) butter

3 Tbsp. (45 mL) flour

1 cup (250 mL) milk

dash of hot-pepper sauce

1/4 tsp. (1 mL) dry mustard

4 Tbsp. (60 mL) finely chopped lovage

1 cup (250 mL) freshly grated aged Cheddar cheese

5 eggs, separated

Preheat oven to 375°F (190°C). Melt butter in a saucepan. Add flour, stirring constantly with a whisk to make a roux. Heat milk in another saucepan, then slowly add to roux, stirring constantly until well blended. Add hot-pepper sauce, mustard and lovage and blend in. Simmer for 2-3 minutes until mixture thickens.

Add cheese and stir until cheese melts and is blended. Remove saucepan from heat and add egg yolks. Stir until well blended and set aside.

Beat egg whites in a bowl until they are stiff. Gently fold egg whites into cheese mixture. Put mixture in a buttered soufflé dish and bake in preheated oven for 35 minutes, until soufflé has risen and set and is light golden brown on top. Serve immediately.

Scandinavian Meatballs with Lovage

Lovage combines well with meat dishes. It cuts the fatty taste and adds a celery flavor to these meatballs. Serve with rice or noodles. Serves 4-6.

2 lbs. (1 kg) ground beef

1/4 lb. (125 g) ground pork

1 egg

freshly ground black pepper

1/4 tsp. (1 mL) ground mace

1/4 tsp. (1 mL) ground ginger

1/2 cup (125 mL) breadcrumbs

2 Tbsp. (30 mL) butter

1/4 cup (50 mL) flour

1 1/2 cups (375 mL) hot water

1 1/2 cups (375 mL) sour cream or yogurt

3 Tbsp. (45 mL) finely chopped lovage

finely chopped lovage, as garnish

Preheat oven to 450°F (230°C). Mix ground beef, ground pork, mace, ginger and breadcrumbs together in a bowl. With wet hands, form mixture into meatballs about the size of golf balls. Place meatballs on a cookie sheet with sides and bake in preheated oven for 10 minutes. Remove cookie sheet from oven and reduce oven heat to 350°F (180°C).

Place meatballs in a casserole dish, and pour drippings from cookie sheet into a skillet. Add butter to skillet and heat. Add flour to skillet, stirring constantly with a whisk to make a roux. Slowly add water to roux, stirring constantly until sauce is thick and smooth. Add sour cream or yogurt and stir until well blended. Add lovage and stir.

Pour sauce over meatballs in casserole dish. Bake for 30 minutes at 350°F (180°C). Garnish with finely chopped lovage.

Marjoram

arjoram is milder in flavor than oregano. It is more subtle and has sweet overtones. It combines well with other herbs and complements pork and tomato dishes. You can use marjoram in spaghetti sauces, or snip it on pizzas. Try it in casseroles or cheese and egg dishes. It is good with roast lamb, lamb chops, or in meatballs. Add it to Béchamel Sauce and use it over vegetables. It is an extremely versatile herb.

Growing

*M*arjoram is a perennial. Similar to oregano in looks, marjoram is a small, shrubby plant of varying habit and hardiness. It interbreeds with oregano and often is difficult to identify. Marjoram needs sun and a moderately fertile, fast-draining soil. It makes a good container plant. Sweet marjoram cannot take any frost and should be grown as an annual.

Quick Ham Pâté with Marjoram

Guests are due to arrive, and all you have on hand is leftover ham. With a blender or food processor, you can have an elegant pâté very quickly! Garnish it with finely chopped marjoram and serve with toast or crackers. Makes 2 cups (500 mL).

2 shallots, finely chopped

3 Tbsp. (45 mL) butter

2 cups (500 mL) chopped cooked ham

2-3 Tbsp. (30-45 mL) chopped marjoram

freshly ground black pepper

1 Tbsp. (15 mL) Dijon mustard

2 Tbsp. (30 mL) brandy

finely chopped marjoram, as garnish

Sauté shallots in butter until limp. Put shallots and remaining ingredients in a food processor and process until smooth. Chill in a small crock until ready to serve.

Freezer Tomato Sauce with Marjoram

In late summer, we make this sauce to use all the ripe tomatoes. Over the winter, we use it as a base for spaghetti sauce, meat loaf sauce, vegetable soups and stews. You can vary the ingredients depending on your harvest. Try making it with basil in place of marjoram or with a combination of the two. Makes 12-15 cups (3-3.75 L).

3 cups (750 mL) chopped onions

4 carrots, peeled and diced

2 cups (500 mL) seeded, chopped green peppers

4 cloves garlic, peeled and crushed

4 Tbsp. (60 mL) vegetable oil

8 lbs. (4 kg) ripe tomatoes, peeled and chopped

1/4 cup (50 mL) finely chopped marjoram

1 bay leaf

freshly ground black pepper

In a large pot, sauté onions, carrots, green peppers and garlic in oil for 5 minutes. Add tomatoes, marjoram, bay leaf and pepper and bring to a boil. Reduce heat to low and simmer for 1 hour, until it is thick and rich-tasting. Cool and freeze in plastic cartons.

Marjoram Herbed Brown Rice with Shallots

The sweet fragrance of marjoram, the gentler cousin of oregano, scents this rice dish. Serve it as a vegetable dish or, with the addition of almonds, pine nuts, cashews, shrimp or pieces of chicken, it can be a main course. Serves 4.

4 shallots, finely chopped

2 cloves garlic, peeled and chopped

4 Tbsp. (60 mL) vegetable oil

1 cup (250 mL) brown rice

2 1/2 cups (625 mL) cold water

1/2 cup (125 mL) raisins

3-4 Tbsp. (45-60 mL) finely chopped marjoram

freshly ground black pepper

In a large saucepan, sauté shallots and garlic in oil for 2-3 minutes. Add rice and sauté for an additional 2 minutes. Add water, raisins, marjoram and pepper and bring to a boil. Reduce heat to low, cover and simmer for 45 minutes, until rice is done. Do not stir rice while cooking. Stir well before serving. Nuts, shrimp or chicken may be added in the last 5 minutes of cooking.

Marjoram Pasta Sauce with Tomatoes and Cheese

Marjoram paired with tomatoes gives a Mediterranean flair to this pasta sauce. Serves 4.

1/2 cup (125 mL) chopped onions

2 carrots, peeled and diced

2 stalks celery, diced

4 Tbsp. (60 mL) vegetable oil

6 ripe tomatoes, peeled and chopped

2 Tbsp. (30 mL) finely chopped marjoram

1 lb. (500 g) cooked pasta

1/2 cup (125 mL) freshly grated Parmesan cheese

freshly grated Parmesan cheese, as garnish

Sauté onions, carrots and celery in 3 Tbsp. (45 mL) of the oil over medium heat for 5 minutes. Reduce heat to low, add tomatoes and simmer for 30 minutes. Put mixture in a blender or food processor and purée. Return mixture to saucepan and add marjoram. Simmer for an additional 10 minutes.

Serve over hot cooked pasta. Sprinkle pasta with remaining 1 Tbsp. (15 mL) oil and 1/2 cup (125 mL) freshly grated Parmesan cheese, then cover with sauce. Toss together well. Serve immediately. At the table, sprinkle with extra Parmesan cheese.

Mediterranean Clam Soup with Marjoram

It is said that the Spanish like the sound of clinking clam shells in their soup bowls. To them, this is true culinary music. Serves 4-6.

2-3 lbs. (1-1.5 kg) fresh clams, washed and scrubbed

2 1/4 cups (550 mL) dry white wine

1 medium onion, chopped

1 stalk celery, chopped

1 leek, washed and finely chopped (use only the white part)

2 cloves garlic, peeled and chopped

3 Tbsp. (45 mL) olive oil

5 cups (1.25 L) fish stock

1 ripe tomato, peeled and chopped

4 Tbsp. (60 mL) finely chopped marjoram

Combine clams and wine in a large pot. Cover pot and steam clams for 5-6 minutes, until their shells open. Drain, reserving liquid. Strain liquid into a bowl, using a sieve lined with a linen or muslin cloth. Leave clams in shells and set aside, discarding any that do not open.

Sauté onion, celery, leek and garlic in oil until onion is limp. Add clam liquid, fish stock, tomato and marjoram and bring to a boil. Gently boil for 10 minutes. Add clams in shells to pot, heat through, and serve immediately.

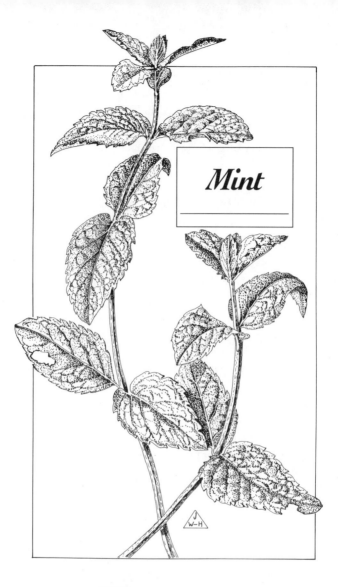

Mint

There is more to mint than mint jelly, although we always make our annual supply of that each fall. Mint is a versatile herb that can be used with meat and vegetables and in salads and desserts. We grow mint in a large Chinese pot just outside the kitchen door so that it can be snipped easily. Chopped mint and yogurt is great on roast chicken. When sautéing zucchini or other fresh vegetables, add a little chopped mint. Chopped mint and sliced cucumbers make a quick, cool salad. Just add a simple oil-and-vinegar dressing. We always include mint in potato salad.

As a child, I was often sent to fetch mint from the garden for new potatoes or peas. This was the beginning of my association with herbs.

Growing

*M*int is a hardy perennial. Like marjoram and oregano, there are many varieties of mint and great confusion over names. You may have to experiment before you find a variety of mint that you like.

Propagation of mint is by division or cuttings. Because of its habit of invasion, mint is best planted in an isolated bed in your garden or in a bottomless container sunk in the ground. Mint likes fairly rich soil and quite a lot of moisture. It can use some shade. Mint makes a good container plant, but it will need dividing and repotting once a year.

Mint Jelly

To some, this jelly is a necessity for lamb chops or roast lamb. Following the recipe for Lemon Balm Jelly (page 63), substitute 2 cups (500 mL) finely chopped mint leaves for the lemon balm.

Mint Sauce

The contrast of vinegar, sugar and mint gives mint sauce its sweet and sour tang. The English have been putting it on their roast lamb since the Middle Ages. Makes 1 cup (250 mL).

1 cup (250 mL) cider vinegar

1/4 cup (50 mL) sugar

1/2 cup (125 mL) finely chopped mint leaves

Put all ingredients in a saucepan and bring to a boil. Remove from heat and cool. Serve with lamb chops or roast lamb.

Cucumber-Mint-Yogurt Soup

A cool soup with a subtle flavor! If you use the long, seedless variety of cucumber, just peel them. Serves 4.

2 medium cucumbers, peeled and seeded

2 cups (500 mL) yogurt

juice of 1/2 lemon

3 Tbsp. (45 mL) chopped mint leaves

freshly ground black pepper

thin slices of lemon and sprigs of mint, as garnish

Purée all ingredients, except garnish, in a blender or food processor. Chill for several hours before serving. Serve ice-cold in soup bowls, each bowl garnished with a thin slice of lemon and a sprig of mint.

Roast Leg of Lamb with Mint Butter

This mint butter can be used for grilled or barbecued lamb chops or breast of lamb as well as roast leg of lamb. Try substituting sage for mint. Serves 6-8.

6 Tbsp. (90 mL) softened butter

4 cloves garlic, peeled and mashed

4 Tbsp. (60 mL) finely chopped mint leaves

freshly ground black pepper

5- to 7-lb. (2.5- to 3.5-kg) leg of lamb

Preheat oven to 325°F (160°C). Mix butter, garlic and mint together in a bowl to form a paste. Season with pepper. Pat paste over leg of lamb. Put lamb in a roasting pan and roast for 1 3/4–2 1/4 hours for rare meat; 2-3 hours for medium meat; and 2 1/2–3 1/2 hours for well-done meat. Use a meat thermometer. It should read 140°F (60°C) for rare meat, 160°F (70°C) for medium meat, and 170-180°F (75-80°F) for well-done meat. Serve roast with homemade mint jelly or mint sauce.

Mint Tea

If you visit Morocco, Algeria or Tunisia, you will constantly come across fresh mint tea. Leftover cold tea can be strained and put in a jar in the refrigerator and used for iced mint tea.

1-2 handfuls mint leaves

several slices of lemon

Put mint leaves in a large teapot and pour boiling water over them. Allow tea to steep for 5 minutes. Serve with a half slice of lemon in each cup. Sweeten with honey.

Oregano

Oregano has a sharper, spicier flavor than marjoram. Although it's widely used as a spaghetti sauce or pizza herb, it has many more uses. It adds flavor to fish and is good with barbecued or broiled lamb and sautéed vegetables such as zucchini. It also makes a delightful herb vinegar.

Growing

*O*regano is a hardy perennial—the sister herb to marjoram. Like marjoram, oregano needs sun and a moderately fertile, fast-draining soil. It makes a good container plant.

Fresh Summer Pizza

The fresh herbs of summer give pizza a more intense flavor. You can use basil, marjoram, Italian parsley or rosemary in place of oregano. Serves 2-3.

13-inch (33-cm) pizza crust

4-6 Tbsp. (60-90 mL) olive oil

5 ripe tomatoes, sliced

5 large mushrooms, cleaned and sliced

4 Tbsp. (60 mL) finely chopped oregano

1/2 cup (125 mL) freshly grated mozzarella cheese

1/2 cup (125 mL) freshly grated Parmesan cheese

Preheat oven to 500°F (260°C). Roll out pizza crust on a board or a flat work surface. Place in oiled pizza pan and spread with fingertips. Brush with oil. Bake crust in preheated oven for 5 minutes.

Remove pan from oven and overlap tomato slices on top of crust. Put mushroom slices over tomato slices. Sprinkle with oregano. Cover with mozzarella and Parmesan cheese. Return pan to oven and bake on lower shelf for 15 minutes, until crust is browned and pizza is bubbly. Serve immediately.

Oregano, Shallot and Mushroom Salad

Marinated salads will keep for several days in the refrigerator and the taste improves. This is a useful emergency salad. Serves 2.

3 cups (750 mL) sliced mushrooms

juice of 1 lemon

1/4 cup (50 mL) finely chopped shallots

cold water (to cover)

2 Tbsp. (30 mL) white wine vinegar

6 Tbsp. (90 mL) olive or vegetable oil

1-2 cloves garlic, peeled and crushed

1/4 cup (50 mL) finely chopped oregano

romaine lettuce leaves

Put sliced mushrooms in a saucepan. Sprinkle with lemon juice. Sprinkle shallots over mushrooms. Add just enough water to cover and bring to a boil. Reduce heat to low and simmer for 5 minutes.

Drain mushrooms and put in a bowl. Add vinegar, oil and garlic. Sprinkle with oregano. Marinate for 2-3 hours in the refrigerator, stirring occasionally. Serve on leaves of romaine lettuce as a first course.

Noël's Eggplant Casserole

When vegetarians come for dinner, I often make this casserole. Steaming the eggplant is speedy and cuts down on the oil that eggplants can soak up like a sponge. Serves 4.

1 medium eggplant, washed and sliced into 1/2-inch-thick (1-cm) rounds

3/4 cup (175 mL) freshly grated mozzarella cheese

4 Tbsp. (60 mL) finely chopped oregano

freshly ground black pepper

1/4 cup (50 mL) freshly grated Parmesan cheese

Preheat oven to 350°F (180°C). Steam eggplant slices in a metal steamer over boiling water for 5 minutes, until fork-tender but not mushy.

Put a layer of eggplant in the bottom of a buttered casserole dish. Cover with a layer of mozzarella cheese, sprinkle with oregano and season with pepper. Repeat until all ingredients are used. Sprinkle Parmesan cheese on top. Bake casserole in preheated oven for 40 minutes, until top is browned and casserole is bubbly. Serve as a main course or as a side dish with meat.

Oregano Oil

Herbal oils liven up salad dressings, and enhance pizzas, barbecued meats, fish and chicken. In this recipe, you can use basil, rosemary or thyme in place of oregano. Herbal oils make good gifts for salad lovers and friends who cook.

4 Tbsp (60 mL) crushed oregano (use a mortar and pestle)

2 cups (500 mL) olive or vegetable oil

Mix oregano and oil together in a cup. Pour into a sterilized bottle. Cap and store in a cool, dark place for 1 week to increase the flavor. If you intend to keep the oil for several months, seal jars with paraffin wax.

Vine Leaves Stuffed with Rice and Oregano

Wrapped food has an exotic charm and it is not difficult to make. Chopped herbs are a natural addition! If you have your own grapevine, you have a great source of food-wrappers. Vine leaves are also available packed in brine. Rinse well before using. Romaine lettuce leaves, sorrel leaves, beet greens, Swiss chard and, of course, the old standby, cabbage, can be used as food-wrappers. The following recipe makes a nice hors d'oeuvre or is a good side dish for a barbecue. Try using basil, chervil, parsley or thyme instead of oregano. Makes 2 dozen.

24 large grapevine leaves

3 cups (750 mL) cooked white or brown rice

2 Tbsp. (30 mL) chopped shallots

1/2 cup (125 mL) finely chopped oregano

1/4 cup (50 mL) raisins

1/4 cup (50 mL) chopped almonds

2 cups (500 mL) hot water

juice of 1 lemon

lemon slices, as garnish

If vine leaves are fresh, pour boiling water over them and let them sit for 5-10 minutes. Mix rice, shallots, oregano, raisins and almonds together in a bowl. Lay each leaf out flat and put 1-2 Tbsp. (15-30 mL) filling on each leaf. Roll up leaves and tuck in ends. Place rolled leaves in a large skillet, and pour hot water over them. Add lemon juice, cover, and simmer over low heat for 25 minutes. Cool and drain. Serve with lemon slices.

Baked Cod with Feta Cheese and Oregano

A combination of salty feta and spicy oregano suits the mild taste of cod. Serve it with rice or boiled new potatoes. Serves 4.

2 lbs. (1 kg) fillet of cod

1/2 cup (125 mL) finely chopped onions

3 cloves garlic, peeled and crushed

2 Tbsp. (30 mL) vegetable oil

4 ripe tomatoes, peeled and chopped

2 Tbsp. (30 mL) tomato paste

2 Tbsp. (30 mL) drained capers

4 Tbsp. (60 mL) finely chopped oregano

1/3 cup (75 mL) finely chopped parsley

freshly ground black pepper

1/4 lb. (125 g) feta cheese, crumbled

finely chopped parsley, as garnish

Preheat oven to 425ºF (220ºC). Lay cod in buttered casserole dish and set aside. Sauté onions and garlic in oil in a skillet over medium heat for 2-3 minutes. Reduce heat to low, add tomatoes, tomato paste, capers, oregano, parsley and pepper and simmer for 8-10 minutes.

Pour contents of skillet over cod in casserole dish. Bake casserole in preheated oven for 15 minutes. Remove from oven and sprinkle with feta cheese. Return to oven and bake for an additional 5 minutes. Just before serving garnish with finely chopped parsley.

Spaghetti with Clams and Oregano

The freshness of this sauce certainly beats canned clams, canned tomatoes and dried herbs! Serves 4.

2-3 lbs. (1-1.5 kg) fresh clams, washed and scrubbed

1/4 cup (50 mL) cold water

2 medium onions, finely chopped

3 cloves garlic, peeled and crushed

3-4 Tbsp. (45-60 mL) vegetable oil

4 ripe tomatoes, peeled and chopped

3 Tbsp. (45 mL) finely chopped oregano

2 Tbsp. (30 mL) finely chopped parsley

freshly ground black pepper

1 lb. (500 g) cooked spaghetti

freshly grated Parmesan cheese (optional)

Steam clams in a large pot with water for 5-6 minutes, until their shells open. Drain, reserving half the liquid. Strain reserved liquid through a sieve lined with a linen or muslin cloth. Remove clams from shells and set aside. Discard any clams that do not open.

In a large skillet, sauté onions and garlic in oil until onions are limp. Add tomatoes, half the oregano and parsley and the reserved clam liquid. Bring to a boil and boil until mixture is reduced by one-half.

Add clams and season with pepper. Heat through, then add sauce to hot cooked spaghetti. Sprinkle with remaining half of oregano and parsley. Toss together well. Serve immediately. Sprinkle with freshly grated Parmesan cheese if you like.

Oregano Chicken Baked in Foil

Each piece of chicken is wrapped in foil, sealing in the taste of the herb. You can use rosemary or tarragon in place of oregano. Serves 4.

2 1/2- to 3 1/2-lb. (1.25- to 1.75-kg) chicken, cut into
   serving pieces

1/4 cup (50 mL) vegetable oil

1/4 cup (50 mL) finely chopped oregano

3 cloves garlic, peeled and crushed

freshly ground black pepper

Preheat oven to 400°F (200°C). Place each piece of chicken on a piece of aluminum foil large enough to wrap the chicken. Brush chicken with oil. Mix oregano, garlic and pepper together in a bowl. Sprinkle some of mixture on each piece of chicken and seal in aluminum foil. Put wrapped chicken in one layer in a baking dish and bake in preheated oven for 45-50 minutes. Remove aluminum foil from chicken and serve.

Parsley

*I*t might seem hard to become excited over parsley. It is always there on your plate when you go out to dinner and often it is not eaten. Yet parsley is a wonderful herb, full of vitamins and minerals. We find it is best-used in food, rather than sitting on the edge of your plate. Parsley makes a quick vegetable dip when mixed with equal amounts of yogurt and mayonnaise. You can add a cup of chopped parsley to your pesto recipe when you are short of basil. Try it in sandwiches, replacing lettuce. It is a great combination herb because of its mild flavor: mix it with other herbs in sauces, soups and stews.

We grow a lot of Italian parsley, as it is a nice change from curly-leafed parsley and it has more flavor. In the recipes in this chapter, you can use the two parsleys interchangeably.

Growing

*P*arsley is a biennial. Both flat-leafed, or Italian, parsley, and the normal curly-leafed parsley require rich soil and frequent watering in dry weather. If cut frequently, fish fertilizer should be watered in every two weeks. Buy plants, or sow seeds after soaking them in water for 48 hours. It is best to sow in place, as only the smallest seedlings are easy to transplant. Sowing in early spring is fine in coastal climates, but seeds can be sown up to early summer for leaves to be picked in early autumn. In areas where the ground freezes, parsley is best treated as an annual. It makes a good container plant when young, but large plants need 10-12 inches (25-30 cm) of soil.

Parsley Butter

A fresh-herb butter that's great on steaks and chops.

4 Tbsp. (60 mL) chopped parsley

a squeeze of anchovy paste

1 Tbsp. (15 mL) freshly squeezed lemon juice

1/4 cup (50 mL) softened butter

freshly ground black pepper

Put all ingredients in a blender or food processor. Process until smooth and chill in a small crock.

Parsley-Shallot Stuffing for Chicken or Cornish Game Hens

The secret of using parsley is to use a lot of it. The shallots add their sweet garlic crunch to the stuffing, which will stuff two Cornish game hens or a 3-lb. (1.75-kg) roasting chicken. Serves 2-3.

4 shallots, finely chopped

4 Tbsp. (60 mL) butter

2 cups (500 mL) fresh breadcrumbs

1 cup (250 mL) finely chopped parsley

chicken stock (to moisten)

freshly ground black pepper

Sauté shallots in butter in a skillet until transparent. Remove skillet from heat. Add breadcrumbs and parsley and mix together. Moisten mixture with enough chicken stock so that stuffing sticks together, but is not soggy. Rinse cavity of chicken or Cornish game hens with cold running water, then pat dry. Sprinkle cavity with pepper. Stuff chicken or hens with stuffing and roast as usual.

Tabouleh with Italian Parsley

Tabouleh is a Middle Eastern salad. It keeps well in the refrigerator for several days and goes well with cold salmon for a buffet lunch in the summertime. Serves 4-6.

2 cups (500 mL) bulgur

4 cups (1 L) finely chopped parsley

1 cup (250 mL) finely chopped mint leaves

1 cup (250 mL) olive oil

1 cup (250 mL) freshly squeezed lemon juice

1 bunch green onions, chopped

3-4 ripe tomatoes, peeled and chopped

freshly ground black pepper

romaine lettuce leaves

Put bulgur in a large bowl and cover with water. Soak bulgur for 30 minutes to 1 hour, until nearly all the water has been absorbed. Drain in a colander and squeeze out any excess water.

Put parsley, mint, oil and lemon juice in a blender or food processor and process in quick spurts until herbs are minced, or mix by hand in a bowl. Add herb mixture to bulgur and mix together. Add onions and tomatoes to bulgur and mix together well. Season with pepper, then refrigerate. Serve tabouleh on romaine lettuce leaves or serve it in a bowl surrounded with romaine lettuce leaves, which can be dipped in the tabouleh.

Parsley Salad

This salad is not boring, so do not leave it on your plate. It tastes good and is also good for you. Serves 4.

2 cups (500 mL) finely chopped parsley

1/2 cup (125 mL) finely chopped red onions

6 Tbsp. (90 mL) olive oil

2 Tbsp. (30 mL) freshly squeezed lemon juice

freshly ground black pepper

Mix all ingredients together in a bowl and serve on lettuce leaves or in a hollowed-out tomato.

Parsley Winter Soup

In temperate climates, parsley keeps growing in the fall and winter. This recipe is a variation of vichyssoise. The soup has a lovely pale green color and is delicious hot or cold. Serves 2-3.

2 cups (500 mL) washed, chopped leeks, or 2 chopped onions

4 Tbsp. (60 mL) butter

4 cups (1 L) chicken stock

6 medium potatoes, peeled and sliced

1 cup (250 mL) finely chopped parsley

freshly ground black pepper

2 cups (500 mL) half-and-half cream

finely chopped parsley, as garnish

Sauté leeks or onions in butter in a skillet for 5 minutes, then set aside. Put chicken stock in a pot and bring to a boil. Add potatoes and cook for 15 minutes. Add leeks or onions and parsley, and season with pepper. Transfer contents of pot to a blender or food processor and purée. Return mixture to pot and add cream. Mix together and heat through. Serve in warm bowls. Garnish with finely chopped parsley on top.

Parsley Green Sauce

This is a great sauce for fish and will keep in the refrigerator for several days. Makes 1 cup (250 mL).

1 large bunch parsley, rinsed, with stalks removed

2 Tbsp. (30 mL) chopped chives or dill

1 medium avocado, pitted and peeled

juice of 1 lemon

1/2 cup (125 mL) cold water

freshly ground black pepper

Purée all ingredients in a blender or food processor. Transfer purée to a bowl, cover and refrigerate until ready to use.

Parsley Potato Pancakes

This is one of my favorite supper dishes. With apple sauce and yogurt, you need nothing else. Substitute 2 cups (500 mL) leftover mashed potatoes for fresh potatoes, or add 1 Tbsp. (15 mL) finely chopped chives or dill for a change. Serves 4.

4 medium potatoes, peeled and grated

2 eggs, beaten

1 cup (250 mL) finely chopped parsley

1/4 cup (50 mL) grated onion

2 Tbsp. (30 mL) flour

vegetable oil for frying

apple sauce and yogurt (optional)

Mix potatoes, eggs, parsley, onion and flour together in a bowl to form a batter. Heat oil over medium heat in a skillet. Drop batter into skillet using a large serving spoon and press pancakes down so that they are thin. Fry pancakes for 2-3 minutes per side until golden brown. Remove from skillet and drain on paper towels. Keep in a warm oven until ready to serve. They are delicious served with apple sauce and yogurt on top.

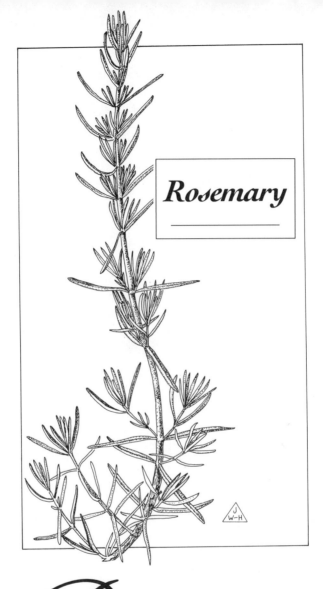

Rosemary

*R*osemary has a strong, piny flavor that is especially good with meat and poultry dishes. Rosemary is one of the few herbs that can be cut and used fresh any month of the year. It is a favorite herb of Italian cooks, who even add it to bread, called foccaccia. For a heavenly scent, throw a few sprigs of rosemary on your barbecue in the summertime.

Growing

*R*osemary is a shrubby perennial. The upright variety is hardy in coastal climates, provided it has good root drainage and some shelter from the wind. The prostrate variety is best used as a container plant and brought in for the winter. Propagation is fairly easy, started from seed in the spring and planted out by midsummer, or from summer cuttings rooted in water, potted up and put in a cool, sunny place for the winter. Six small plants or one large plant is enough for a small family.

Rosemary Marinade for Meats

Use this marinade with pork, lamb, veal or venison. This is enough marinade for 4 steaks, a small roast or a cut-up chicken.

2 cups (500 mL) dry red wine

1/2 cup (125 mL) vegetable oil

1/4 cup (50 mL) red wine vinegar

2 medium onions, chopped

1 cup (250 mL) chopped celery

2-3 cloves garlic, peeled and crushed

2 Tbsp. (30 mL) chopped rosemary

freshly ground black pepper

Mix ingredients in a saucepan and bring to a boil. Put meat in a glass, ceramic, or enamel dish and pour marinade over top. Cover and refrigerate for at least 24 hours. Cook meat as usual. Cook marinade until it's reduced to about 1/2-1 cup (125-250 mL), to make a sauce.

Roast Lamb with Rosemary

This is the classic French way of cooking lamb. As we raise sheep and have a herb farm, guests often have this for dinner. Serves 6-8.

3- to 5-lb. (1.5- to 2.5-kg) shoulder of lamb, or 5- to 7-lb.

   (2.5- to 3.5-kg) leg of lamb

4 cloves garlic, peeled and slivered

3 Tbsp. (45 mL) rosemary leaves

freshly ground black pepper

Preheat oven to 325°F (160°C). Make slits in shoulder or leg of lamb. Insert garlic and rosemary in slits. Lamb should be studded with garlic and rosemary. Season with pepper. Roast lamb for 1 3/4-2 1/4 hours for rare meat. Thermometer should read 140°F (60°C) for rare meat, which is how the French like their lamb.

Rosemary Potato Casserole

Over the years, rosemary has become my first-choice herb for potato dishes. The piny, peppery taste lifts potatoes into a new realm. Serves 4-6.

2 lbs. (1 kg) potatoes, peeled and sliced

4 tsp. (20 mL) chopped rosemary leaves

1/2 cup (125 mL) butter

freshly ground black pepper

1 cup (250 mL) milk or half-and-half cream

Preheat oven to 375°F (190°C). Layer potatoes and rosemary in a casserole dish. Dot with butter and season with pepper. Repeat until ingredients are all used. Pour milk or cream over top.

   Cover and bake in preheated oven for 1 hour. Uncover and bake for an additional 30 minutes until browned. Serve hot.

Rosemary Scallops

The mild scallops and brisk taste of rosemary make a surprisingly good combination. Serve this dish with rice. Serves 4-5.

2 lbs. (1 kg) fresh scallops

1/2 cup (125 mL) half-and-half cream

1/4 cup (50 mL) dry white wine

2 tsp. (10 mL) freshly squeezed lemon juice

1 Tbsp. (15 mL) finely chopped shallots

2 Tbsp. (30 mL) chopped rosemary leaves

freshly ground black pepper

3/4 cup (175 mL) fine breadcrumbs

4 Tbsp. (60 mL) butter

Preheat oven to 450°F (230°C). Put scallops in buttered casserole dish. Mix cream, wine, lemon juice, shallots and rosemary together in a bowl. Season with pepper. Pour mixture over scallops in casserole dish. Cover with breadcrumbs and dot with butter. Put casserole dish in preheated oven and bake uncovered for 10-12 minutes. Increase heat to broil/grill to brown topping.

Roast Veal with Rosemary

Cook this veal in a clay pot—it will be succulent and full of flavor. It can also be cooked in a regular casserole dish or a Dutch oven. Serves 4-6.

4 Tbsp. (60 mL) olive oil

3- to 4-lb. (1.5- to 2-kg) boneless roast of veal

2-3 cloves garlic, peeled and crushed

3 Tbsp. (45 mL) finely chopped rosemary leaves

1 cup (250 mL) dry white vermouth

freshly ground black pepper

If using a clay cooker, soak pot and lid in cold water for 15 minutes, then pat dry. Heat oil in a skillet and brown roast on all sides. Add garlic and rosemary to skillet while browning. Put roast in clay pot or casserole dish.

Add vermouth to skillet and bring to a boil, scraping up pan drippings. Season with pepper. Pour contents of skillet over roast and cover pot with lid. Bake in oven at 325°F (160°C) for 2 1/2 hours.

If desired, put peeled onions, mushrooms, carrots and small potatoes around roast during last hour of cooking. To serve, carve roast into slices, and pour pan juices over top.

Rosemary Meat Loaf

If you have any leftover meat loaf, it is good cold for lunch the next day—or try it in sandwiches. The rosemary gives the meat loaf a unique flavor. Serves 4-6.

1 1/2 lbs. (700 g) ground beef

2 eggs, beaten

4 shallots, finely chopped

1 Tbsp. (15 mL) finely chopped rosemary leaves

freshly ground black pepper

1/4 cup (50 mL) chili sauce

2 Tbsp. (30 mL) brown sugar

1 Tbsp. (15 mL) Dijon mustard

Preheat oven to 350°F (180°C). Mix ground beef, eggs, shallots and rosemary together in a bowl. Season with pepper. Pat mixture into a loaf pan. Mix chili sauce, sugar and mustard together in another bowl and spread over meat loaf. Put loaf pan in preheated oven and bake for 1 hour.

Rosemary Chicken

This is an Italian way of cooking chicken, which turns golden brown and is redolent of rosemary. You can use this method to cook a smaller frying chicken or a Cornish game hen. Serves 4-6.

4-lb. (2-kg) roasting chicken

2 cloves garlic, peeled and left whole

4 Tbsp. (60 mL) rosemary leaves

freshly ground black pepper

1/4 cup (50 mL) olive or vegetable oil

2 cloves garlic, peeled and chopped

1/4 cup (50 mL) dry white vermouth

Preheat oven to 375°F (190°C). Rinse chicken inside and out under cold running water and pat dry. Put chicken in a roasting pan. Put 2 whole cloves garlic and half the rosemary in cavity of chicken. Season with pepper.

Rub half the oil on skin of chicken. Sprinkle chicken with chopped garlic, remaining half of rosemary and season with pepper. Pour remaining half of oil in bottom of roasting pan. Put roasting pan in preheated oven and bake for 1 hour, basting every 15 minutes.

When chicken is done, remove roasting pan from oven. Remove chicken to serving platter and keep warm. Skim fat from roasting pan. Add vermouth to pan and cook, scraping up pan juices. Carve chicken into slices and pour pan juices over top.

Rosemary Jelly

Follow the recipe for Lemon Balm Jelly (page 63), using 4 Tbsp. (60 mL) rosemary leaves and a few drops of red food coloring instead of lemon balm and yellow food coloring.

Sage

One French chef we know snorts at the mention of sage and calls it "that English herb." But it is not just the English who use sage—Italians, for instance, have found many uses for it in their cooking. Most people think of sage as the dried herb that you add to turkey stuffing. But fresh sage is another matter—it is emphatic, robust, not at all bitter-tasting, and it can be used in many ways. You will never miss salt in a recipe when you are using sage. Sage butter is great with game or rubbed on roast pork. Sage jelly is good with meat loaf, chops or sausages. Add a little chopped sage to fried chicken; put some in cheese baking-powder biscuits or sausage quiche; sprinkle a little in hamburger meat or on Italian foccaccia bread. Once when we were driving through the outskirts of Siena in Italy, we looked into the backyards of the houses and they nearly all had sage and rosemary bushes growing in their gardens.

Growing

*G*arden sage (salvia officinalis) is a shrubby perennial that is hardy to 10°F (-12°C). It needs well-drained, not too rich soil and is easily propagated by seed, cuttings and layering. Sage is not a good container plant, except when young, but it can be overwintered in a container in a cool greenhouse or on a sunny, sheltered balcony. Lime is normally added to the soil when growing sage in coastal climates.

Sage Jelly

Follow the recipe for Lemon Balm Jelly (page 62), substituting 4 Tbsp. (60 mL) finely chopped sage for the lemon balm and a few drops of yellow food coloring for the green.

Saltimbocca

Saltimbocca in Italian means "leap into your mouth." Need we say more? Serves 4.

8 2-oz. (50-g) slices of veal, pounded thin

8 1-oz. (30-g) slices lean ham

8 large whole leaves of sage

freshly ground black pepper

1/4 cup (50 mL) butter

2 Tbsp. (30 mL) olive oil

5 Tbsp. (75 mL) dry white wine

On each slice of veal, place 1 slice of ham and 1 leaf of sage. Season with pepper. Roll slices of veal and secure with a toothpick. Sauté veal rolls in butter and oil in a skillet for 3-4 minutes until browned. Add wine to skillet and simmer for 12 minutes. Use the pan drippings as a sauce, and serve with pan-roasted potatoes.

Green Beans with Sage

Green beans get a new lease on life with fresh sage and Parmesan. Serves 4.

1 lb. (500 g) green beans, trimmed

2 Tbsp. (30 mL) butter

1/4 cup (50 mL) freshly grated Parmesan cheese

1 Tbsp. (15 mL) finely chopped sage

freshly ground black pepper

Steam beans in a metal or Chinese bamboo steamer for 5 minutes, or boil until just tender. Melt butter in saucepan. Add cheese and sage and mix together. Season with pepper. Toss beans in mixture until they are coated, and serve immediately.

Creamed Onions with Sage

A delicious side dish with roast chicken, duck, pheasant or goose. Serves 4.

8 small-medium onions, peeled and left whole

3 Tbsp. (45 mL) butter

4 Tbsp. (60 mL) flour

1 1/2 cups (375 mL) milk

freshly ground black pepper

1 Tbsp. (15 mL) finely chopped sage

1/2 cup (125 mL) fine breadcrumbs

3 Tbsp. (45 mL) butter

Preheat oven to 350°F (180°C). Put onions in a saucepan and cover with water. Bring to a boil and cook for 10-12 minutes until tender. Drain, reserving 1/2 cup (125 mL) cooking liquid.

Melt butter in a saucepan. Add flour, stirring constantly with a whisk to make a roux. Slowly add milk to saucepan and bring to a boil, stirring constantly with a whisk until mixture thickens. Season with pepper. Add reserved cooking liquid to saucepan and blend in. Add sage and stir.

Put onions in buttered casserole dish and cover with sauce. Sprinkle with breadcrumbs and dot with butter. Bake in a preheated oven for 20 minutes until browned and bubbly.

Sage Three-Liver Pâté

*Three different kinds of liver and sage give this pâté a robust
flavor. With a food processor, this recipe is not hard to make.
In place of sage, you can use rosemary or thyme or a combination
of these herbs. This is a good recipe to make a day or two ahead of
time. Serve it with French bread, toast or crackers. Makes 1 loaf
pan.*

1/2 lb. (250 g) sliced bacon

1/2 lb. (250 g) calf liver

1/2 lb. (250 g) pork liver

1/2 lb. (250 g) chicken liver

4 shallots, chopped

3-4 cloves garlic, peeled and chopped

1 egg, beaten

1/4 cup (50 mL) brandy

1 Tbsp. (15 mL) finely chopped sage

freshly ground black pepper

Preheat oven to 325°F (160°C). Line a loaf pan with strips of
bacon. Grind calf, pork and chicken livers, shallots and garlic in a
food processor. Add egg, brandy and sage and mix together.
Season with pepper. Transfer mixture to prepared loaf pan and
cover with aluminum foil. Put loaf pan in a pan of boiling water
and place in a preheated oven. Bake for 1 1/2 hours. Remove from
oven, cool and cover with plastic wrap. Place a 2-lb. (1-kg) weight
on top of covered pâté in loaf pan and refrigerate until ready to
serve.

Roast Duck with Sage and Apple Stuffing

Childhood memories come flooding back when I make this recipe. My mother raised ducks and this is a version of her stuffing recipe. It goes well with wild or domestic duck—its rich flavor matches the gamy taste of duck. Serves 2-3.

4 shallots, finely chopped

4 Tbsp. (60 mL) butter

4 cups (1 L) fresh breadcrumbs

3 medium-sized tart apples, peeled, cored and chopped

1 Tbsp. (15 mL) finely chopped sage

freshly ground black pepper

1 chicken bouillon cube, dissolved in 1/2 cup (125 mL)
    boiling water

3- to 4-lb. (1.5 to 2-kg) duck, ready to cook

4 Tbsp. (60 mL) softened butter

Preheat oven to 350°F (180°C). Sauté shallots in butter in a skillet for 3-4 minutes. In a bowl, mix together shallots, breadcrumbs, apple and sage. Season with pepper and add enough bouillon dissolved in water to just moisten mixture: stuffing should not be soggy.

Rinse duck inside and out under cold water and pat dry. Stuff cavity of duck with stuffing. Do not pack—stuffing expands during cooking. Rub skin of duck with softened butter and put duck in a roasting pan. Prick skin with the tines of a fork. Bake in preheated oven for 1 1/2 hours or until done. Skim fat from pan and make a gravy from pan juices. This duck goes well with mashed potatoes and cooked red cabbage.

Summer
& Winter
Savory

Summer savory is sweeter than the spicy winter savory. Winter savory has the strong flavor of sage or thyme. We use it more in the wintertime, when we cook heavier dishes such as soups, stews and baked beans. The more delicate sister herb, summer savory, we use in the summertime, since it does not last when the cool fall weather comes.

Both savories enhance vegetable dishes, particularly any kind of beans. Some people grow summer savory right beside their bean rows so that they can gather the two together. When steaming or boiling beans, throw in a few sprigs of summer savory. Cook broad beans with a few sprigs of winter savory. Add summer savory to cold bean salads, and to the dressing for the salad. Stuffed mushrooms are delicious with breadcrumbs, freshly grated Parmesan cheese and either of the savories. Snip a few leaves of summer savory over chicken as it is barbecuing, and use winter savory in marinades for cooking meats.

Growing

Summery savory is an annual. Sow in place in rich soil in late spring. Water every two or three days in dry weather. Summer savory can be container-grown, but it becomes rather straggly by the fall.

Winter savory is a shrubby, hardy perennial. Stronger in flavor than summery savory, it grows more slowly. It needs light garden soil and full sun. Propagation is by seed, cuttings, layering or division of older plants. Winter savory is an attractive-looking herb and it makes a good container plant.

Green Beans
with Summer Savory and Crème Fraîche

Serve this at a summer dinner party. Crème Fraîche is a useful sauce that's easy to make, but impossible to buy unless you live in France. It's great on vegetables of all kinds—snow peas, zucchini or summer squash. It thickens sauces well and, when sweetened, is delicious with dessert. Serves 4.

1 lb. (500 g) green beans, trimmed

1 Tbsp. (15 mL) finely chopped summer savory

1/2 cup (125 mL) Crème Fraîche (recipe follows)

Steam beans in a metal or Chinese bamboo steamer for 5 minutes, or boil until just tender. Add savory to beans. Toss beans in Crème Fraîche, and serve immediately.

Crème Fraîche

2 cups (500 mL) whipping cream

1 cup (250 mL) yogurt

Mix cream and yogurt together in a bowl. Let mixture sit at room temperature for 6-8 hours. It will get thick and have a yogurtlike flavor. Crème Fraîche keeps in the refrigerator for several days.

Pork Chops with Apples and Winter Savory

The fruity sauce with the sharp tang of savory goes well with pork. Serve the pork chops on a bed of rice and spoon sauce over chops and rice before serving. Serves 4.

2 medium onions, chopped

4 Tbsp. (60 mL) vegetable oil

3 tart apples, peeled, cored and sliced

4 6-oz. (175-g) pork chops, approximately 1 inch (2.5 cm) thick

2 Tbsp. (30 mL) flour

3 Tbsp. (45 mL) brown sugar

1 Tbsp. (15 mL) finely chopped winter savory

1 1/2 cups (375 mL) cold water or chicken stock

freshly ground black pepper

Sauté onions in oil for 3-5 minutes, then remove from skillet and set aside. Sauté apples in same skillet for 5 minutes, then remove from skillet and set aside. Dust pork chops with flour, and sauté in skillet for 3 minutes per side until browned. Add extra oil to skillet if needed. Sprinkle sugar and savory on top of each pork chop, then cover with onion and apple slices. Season with pepper.

Add water or chicken stock to skillet and simmer over medium-low heat for 20-25 minutes. Sauce will thicken. Add more water or chicken stock to skillet if it evaporates too quickly.

Sorrel

orrel is a lemony, spinachlike herb which
grows for most of the year in coastal climates
and thrives on being picked. Its pale green
color adds visual delight to your food and its piquant flavor
brightens soups, salads, sauces and mild fish dishes. Snip some

sorrel into a spring salad. Add a few finely chopped leaves to your vinaigrette dressing recipe. Put a few leaves in the middle of an omelette. Add a few tablespoons (mL) to lunchtime cottage cheese or sprinkle it over cream cheese sandwiches. Wrap sorrel leaves around a whole salmon or a roast of pork and cook in aluminum foil. When you start using sorrel, you will understand why it is a great standby in French cooking.

Growing

*S*orrel is a leafy perennial. French sorrel (*rumex scutatus*) has wider leaves, is milder in flavor and is less acidic than wild sorrel. It needs rich, fairly most soil and can be propagated either from seed in the spring or summer or from division of old plants in the early spring. If plants are kept well watered, they will only need fertilizing (with fish fertilizer) when the leaf size decreases markedly. It is important to cut off all flowering stalks close to the ground to ensure a continuing supply of new leaves. Continue cutting off flower stalks all summer. Young seedlings are fine as container plants, but old plants develop massive root systems and will not fit in small containers.

Baked Salmon Noël

Wrapping the salmon in sorrel leaves makes it very moist and gives it a lemony flavor. Serves 6-8.

4- to 6-lb. (2- to 3-kg) salmon, cleaned, with the head removed

4 Tbsp. (60 mL) olive oil

freshly ground black pepper

4-6 cups (1-1.5 L) washed sorrel leaves

sorrel leaves, lemon slices and sprigs of parsley, as garnish

Preheat oven to 350ºF (180ºC). Wash salmon and pat dry. Lay fish on a large piece of aluminum foil. Brush with oil. Season interior of salmon with pepper and stuff with sorrel leaves. Cover outside of salmon with sorrel leaves and wrap tightly in foil.

Put fish in a baking pan and bake for 1 hour in preheated oven. Test for doneness: when fish is done, it should flake, but it should be firm and moist. Depending on thickness, you may need to bake it for an additional 10-15 minutes.

When fish is cooked, unwrap and discard sorrel leaves. Serve fish on a warm platter, garnished with sorrel leaves, lemon slices and sprigs of parsley. Serve with Sorrel Sauce (page 112), lemon butter or Blender Hollandaise Sauce (page 120).

Sorrel Salad Dressing

Delicious on tomatoes, tuna salad or chicken! Makes 3/4 cup (175 mL).

1/2 cup (125 mL) washed sorrel leaves

1/4 cup (50 mL) yogurt

1/4 cup (50 mL) half-and-half cream

2 Tbsp. (30 mL) cream cheese

1 Tbsp. (15 mL) freshly squeezed lemon juice

Put all ingredients in a blender or food processor and purée. Transfer to a bowl and chill in refrigerator until ready to serve. Garnish with finely chopped sorrel leaves and serve separate from salad. Toss salad with dressing at the table.

Steamed Sole with Sorrel

In place of sole, you can use halibut, cod or red snapper in this recipe. Served with brown rice, this is a healthy, hearty meal. Use a Chinese bamboo steamer for steaming. Serves 4.

4 cups (1 L) washed sorrel leaves

4 large fillets of sole

freshly ground black pepper

4 Tbsp. (60 mL) melted butter

Line a Chinese bamboo steamer with half the sorrel leaves. Put sole on top of leaves and season with pepper. Put another layer of leaves on top of sole, reserving 3 or 4 leaves. Steam fish over boiling water for 10 minutes, or until fish flakes easily.
Chop reserved sorrel leaves into very fine strips. Add to melted butter. Just before serving, pour butter mixture over fish.

Sorrel Sauce

A useful sauce for veal, pork, noodles or eggs—it turns poached eggs into Eggs Sorrel Benedict! Makes 1 1/2 cups (375 mL).

2 cups (500 mL) washed sorrel leaves

1 1/4 cups (300 mL) chicken or fish stock

1 Tbsp. (15 mL) butter

1 Tbsp. (15 mL) flour

1/4 cup (50 mL) half-and-half cream

freshly ground black pepper

Cook sorrel in chicken or fish stock in a saucepan for 5 minutes, then purée mixture in a blender or food processor.
Melt butter in a saucepan and add flour, stirring constantly with a whisk to make a roux. Slowly add puréed sorrel mixture to roux, stirring constantly with a whisk until well-blended. Simmer for 4-5 minutes. Add cream and blend in. Season with pepper. Heat through before serving.

Sorrel Soup

There are many versions of this soup. In winter, we make a potato-based sorrel soup that is fortifying. In spring, we make a soup that is half-spinach, half-sorrel, which is a true spring tonic. The following is our recipe for spring Sorrel Soup. Serve it cold on a warm evening. It is a refreshing way to start a dinner party. Serves 4.

4 cups (1 L) washed sorrel leaves

4 cups (1 L) washed spinach leaves

4 shallots, finely chopped, or 1 medium onion, finely chopped

4 Tbsp. (60 mL) butter

2 cups (500 mL) chicken stock

1 1/2 cups (375 mL) half-and-half cream

freshly ground black pepper

chopped chives and lemon slices, as garnish

Cook sorrel and spinach in a saucepan with very little water until limp. Drain and purée in a blender or food processor. Set aside.

Sauté shallots or onion in butter in a saucepan for 3-4 minutes. Add chicken stock and bring to a boil. Reduce heat to low and simmer for 5 minutes.

Add puréed sorrel and spinach to stock and mix together, stirring constantly with a whisk until smooth. Add cream to mixture and blend in. Season with pepper.

Serve hot or cold. Chill well for cold soup. Garnish with chopped chives and a slice of lemon in the centre of each bowl of soup.

Sorrel-Spinach Purée

Purées are sophisticated nursery food. Sorrel makes this purée tart and lemony; it can be used as a side vegetable, or tucked into a soufflé or omelette. Serves 4.

4 cups (1 L) washed sorrel leaves

4 cups (1 L) washed spinach leaves

2 Tbsp. (30 mL) butter

1/4 cup (50 mL) half-and-half cream

1 egg, beaten

2 Tbsp. (30 mL) freshly squeezed lemon juice

freshly ground black pepper

Cook sorrel and spinach in a saucepan with very little water until limp. Drain and purée in a blender or food processor. Melt butter in a saucepan. Add puréed mixture to saucepan, then add cream, egg and lemon juice and mix together, stirring constantly with a whisk until smooth. Season with pepper. Heat through, then serve.

Tarragon

*I*f we could take only one herb to grow on a desert island, it would be difficult to choose between basil and tarragon. The sight of the first tarragon in the spring means we can make fresh tarragon chicken. The anise flavor of tarragon is much more gentle and subtle when cooked than it is raw. Chew on a piece of tarragon when you are weeding your garden and it will keep you alert! Add a little chopped tarragon to your favorite oil-and-vinegar dressing or add it to basic Blender Mayonnaise (page 16). As you use tarragon more and more, you will probably find that it becomes a vital part of cooking with seafood. It is a favorite of French cooks and rightfully deserves the title "Queen of Herbs."

Growing

*T*arragon is a perennial that is hardy to -20°F (-29°C), provided soil drainage is excellent. Don't confuse it with Russian tarragon, which looks similar, but has no flavor.

French tarragon does not seed. It needs moderately rich soil, and old plants benefit from fish fertilizer in the summertime if they are being cut heavily.

Two to three large plants are enough for a small family. The best way to propagate it is by carefully dividing plants in the early spring, making sure that each division has roots and stem growth points. Plants with restricted root space tend to lose flavor after three to four years. Young plants can be container-grown, but they need a lot of root room. Tarragon needs a cold, dormant period in the early winter and is more suited to a cool greenhouse than house temperatures.

Tarragon Chicken

There are many versions of this recipe. This uses a whole roasting chicken, but you could easily use pieces of chicken or Cornish game hens. It is a lovely dish if you are having company over for Sunday dinner. The chicken is moist and flavorful and the sauce is smooth and creamy. Serves 4-6.

3- to 4-lb. (1.5- to 2-kg) roasting chicken

1/2 cup (125 mL) softened butter

6 Tbsp. (90 mL) finely chopped tarragon

freshly ground black pepper

sprigs of tarragon

2 Tbsp. (30 mL) butter

2 Tbsp. (30 mL) flour

3/4 cup (175 mL) whipping cream

Preheat oven to 375°F (190°C). Rinse chicken inside and out under cold running water and pat dry. Cream 1/2 cup (125 mL) butter with 4 Tbsp. (60 mL) of the tarragon and season with pepper. Put half of the herb butter inside the chicken with a few sprigs of tarragon.

Put chicken in a roasting pan. Pat remaining half of herb butter on skin of chicken. Bake for 1 1/2 hours, basting occasionally, until chicken is browned. When chicken is done, remove roasting pan from oven and place chicken on a serving platter. Keep chicken warm while making the sauce.

Melt 2 Tbsp. (30 mL) butter in a saucepan. Add remaining 2 Tbsp. (30 mL) tarragon and the flour, stirring constantly with a whisk to make a roux. Add cream, stirring constantly until sauce is thick and smooth. Add pan juices and drippings to saucepan, stirring until smooth and sauce is heated through. Pour into a jug and serve on the side.

Clear Tarragon Soup

This simple, light soup has a strong tarragon flavor. Serves 4.

4 cups (1 L) chicken stock

4-6 Tbsp. (60-90 mL) finely chopped tarragon

freshly ground black pepper

4 Tbsp. (60 mL) freshly grated Parmesan cheese

finely chopped tarragon, as garnish

Simmer chicken stock, tarragon and pepper in a saucepan for 10 minutes. Just before serving, add Parmesan cheese and stir. Serve in bowls garnished with finely chopped tarragon.

Creamy Tarragon Dressing

Tarragon gives the mayonnaise its summery anise flavor. I like to serve it with tomatoes, hard-boiled eggs or cold seafood.
Makes 2 cups (500 mL).

1 cup (250 mL) mayonnaise

1/2 cup (125 mL) milk

1/4 cup (50 mL) vegetable oil

2 Tbsp. (30 mL) white wine vinegar

2 cloves garlic, peeled and crushed

2 Tbsp. (30 mL) finely chopped tarragon

1/2 tsp. (2 mL) curry powder

Put all ingredients in a blender or food processor and blend until smooth. Chill in the refrigerator for several hours to increase the flavor.

Tarragon Fish Sauce

Serve with sole, halibut, cod, red snapper or salmon. The mixture of tarragon and lemon juice gives this sauce its zest. Makes 1 cup (250 mL).

3 Tbsp. (45 mL) butter

2/3 cup (150 mL) whipping cream

3 Tbsp. (45 mL) finely chopped tarragon

1 Tbsp. (15 mL) freshly squeezed lemon juice

freshly ground black pepper

Melt butter in a saucepan. Add cream and simmer until cream has thickened. Add tarragon and lemon juice and stir. Season with pepper. Heat gently for 2-3 minutes. Pour over cooked fish.

Tarragon Blender Béarnaise

A classic sauce that's great over steaks, roast beef and even the lowly hamburger. Makes about 1 cup (250 mL).

1/4 cup (50 mL) tarragon vinegar

2 Tbsp. (30 mL) minced shallots

2 Tbsp. (30 mL) finely chopped tarragon

1/4 tsp. (1 mL) white pepper

3 large egg yolks

1 cup (250 mL) melted butter, cooled slightly

Mix vinegar, shallots, tarragon and pepper together in a small saucepan. Cook over high heat until mixture has reduced to 1-2 Tbsp. (15-30 mL). Transfer contents of saucepan to blender or food processor. Add egg yolks and process briefly. With machine running, slowly add cooled melted butter in a steady stream and blend until mixture thickens. Serve immediately or keep warm over hot water.

Tarragon Blender Hollandaise

This is our favorite sauce with baked salmon. It can also be used on other seafood or on vegetables, egg dishes and crêpes. In place of tarragon, you can use basil, chervil or chives. Makes 2 cups (500 mL).

3 egg yolks

1 1/2 Tbsp. (20 mL) freshly squeezed lemon juice

1 Tbsp. (15 mL) hot water

3/4 cup (175 mL) melted butter

3 Tbsp. (45 mL) finely chopped tarragon

1 tsp. (5 mL) Dijon mustard

dash of cayenne

Put egg yolks and lemon juice in a blender or food processor and blend. Add hot water to mixture and blend. With machine running, slowly add melted butter in a steady stream and blend until mixture thickens. Add tarragon, mustard and cayenne and blend briefly. Serve at room temperature. If reheating, heat slowly over hot water.

Tarragon Vinegar

This is the best-selling vinegar at the farm. I use it for vinaigrettes, marinades, pickles, and to splash into sauces for a tarragon lift. Makes 4 cups (1 L).

4 cups (1 L) boiling red or white wine vinegar

2 cups (500 mL) loosely packed sprigs of tarragon

Place tarragon in a crock or glass container and cover with boiling vinegar. Cover and allow mixture to steep in a cool, dark place for 2 weeks. Strain vinegar into a saucepan; discard tarragon.

Wash and sterilize your bottles. Bring vinegar to a boil and pour into bottles. Add a sprig of tarragon to each bottle. Cap bottles and store in a cool, dark place.

Poached Cod with Puréed Vegetable Sauce

The puréed vegetables make a tasty sauce for the cod. Serve this dish over rice and sprinkle with chopped tarragon. Serves 4.

2 lbs. (1 kg) cod, cut into cubes

2-3 Tbsp. (30-45 mL) olive oil

2 Tbsp. (30 mL) butter

1 medium onion, chopped

2 Tbsp. (30 mL) chopped shallots

2 cloves garlic, peeled and crushed

3 cups (750 mL) peeled, chopped ripe tomatoes

1/4 cup (50 mL) chopped carrots

1/4 cup (50 mL) chopped celery

1 cup (250 mL) dry white wine

3 Tbsp. (45 mL) finely chopped tarragon

1 Tbsp. (15 mL) finely chopped thyme

1 bay leaf

dash of cayenne

Sauté cod in oil for 1 minute. Add butter to cod in skillet, then add remaining ingredients and bring to a boil. Reduce heat to medium-low and poach fish and vegetables for 8 minutes.

Spoon cod from skillet and set aside. Discard bay leaf. Transfer contents of skillet to a blender or food processor and purée. Return puréed vegetable mixture to skillet. Add cod and heat through.

Quick Broiled Sole with Tarragon Butter

A versatile herb butter that's great on fish, vegetables and French bread. Remember, you can freeze herb butters until you want to use them. You can also try this with chives or fennel. Serves 4.

4 Tbsp. (60 mL) finely chopped tarragon

4 Tbsp. (60 mL) softened butter

2 Tbsp. (30 mL) freshly squeezed lemon juice

4 large fillets of sole

freshly ground black pepper

lemon slices and sprigs of tarragon, as garnish

Preheat oven to broil/grill. Mash tarragon and butter together in a bowl. Add lemon juice and blend in.

Put sole in a baking dish. Spread butter over sole. Season with pepper. Broil/grill for 3-5 minutes per side, depending on thickness of fish. Remove from oven. Garnish with lemon slices and sprigs of tarragon and serve immediately.

Sole Stuffed with Crab and Tarragon

This dish is a special way to prepare sole. Serve it with parsleyed new potatoes and use the pan juices as a sauce. Serves 4.

4 large fillets of sole

1/2 lb. (250 g) crab meat

1 egg yolk

2 Tbsp. (30 mL) fine breadcrumbs

4 Tbsp. (60 mL) melted butter

2 Tbsp. (30 mL) finely chopped tarragon

freshly ground black pepper

2 Tbsp. (30 mL) finely chopped shallots

1/2 cup (125 mL) dry white vermouth

Preheat oven to 375°F (190°C). Put 2 fillets of sole in a buttered baking dish. Mix crab meat, egg yolk, breadcrumbs, butter and tarragon together in a bowl. Season with pepper. Evenly spread crab mixture over sole in baking dish. Cover with remaining 2 fillets and press down. Sprinkle shallots around sole in baking dish.

Put vermouth in a saucepan and bring to a boil. Pour vermouth over sole. Cover baking dish with aluminum foil. Bake for 25 minutes in preheated oven. Serve hot.

Tarragon Scallops

This recipe takes only minutes to prepare, yet the results are excellent. Tarragon and delicate scallops are good companions. Serves 2.

1 lb. (500 g) fresh scallops

1/4 cup (50 mL) milk

1/4 cup (50 mL) flour

freshly ground black pepper

5 Tbsp. (75 mL) vegetable oil

4 Tbsp. (60 mL) butter

juice of 1/2 lemon

3 Tbsp. (45 mL) finely chopped tarragon

2 Tbsp. (30 mL) finely chopped parsley

Soak scallops in milk for a few minutes. Mix flour and pepper together. Remove scallops from milk and lightly dredge them in flour, shaking off the excess. Sauté scallops in oil until browned. Remove scallops from skillet and set aside. Discard oil from skillet.

Add butter to skillet, then add lemon juice, tarragon and parsley and cook until butter begins to bubble. Return scallops to skillet and heat through. Serve over cooked pasta or rice.

Cod with Tarragon and Shallots

I learned this unique, easy method of cooking a whole fish in a Chinese cooking class. To complete the meal, serve with rice and stir-fried vegetables. Serves 2-3.

2- to 3-lb. (1- to 1.5-kg) small rock cod, cleaned,
    with the head on

3 Tbsp. (45 mL) finely chopped shallots or green onions

4-5 Tbsp. (60-75 mL) butter

4 Tbsp. (60 mL) finely chopped tarragon

lemon wedges, sprigs of parsley and tarragon, as garnish

Fill a large pot with enough water to cover entire fish and bring to a boil. Remove pot from heat. Put fish in pot, cover and set aside for 15 minutes. Remove fish from water, drain, and place on a warm platter. Fish is done when it separates into firm chunks.

Sauté shallots or green onions in butter in a saucepan. Add tarragon and simmer for 1-2 minutes. Pour butter sauce over fish; garnish with sprigs of parsley and tarragon and lemon wedges.

Herbed Shrimp Fry

A quick-fix lunch—the results look beautiful and taste great! Serves 2-3.

1 lb. (500 g) raw shrimp or prawns, peeled

3 Tbsp. (45 mL) olive oil

2 cloves garlic, peeled and crushed

4 Tbsp. (60 mL) finely chopped tarragon

4 Tbsp. (60 mL) finely chopped parsley

2 Tbsp. (30 mL) freshly squeezed lemon juice

Sauté shrimp or prawns in oil for 3-4 minutes, stirring constantly. Add garlic, tarragon, parsley and lemon juice and simmer for 3 minutes. Serve it on toast with a green salad.

English &
Lemon Thyme

*T*hyme grows all year round in coastal climates, so it is a good friend to cooks. It can be used in heavier dishes in the wintertime and in light dishes in the summertime. Snip some lemon thyme into a saucepan when you are cooking green beans or zucchini. Make a herb jelly with either thyme. Lemon thyme butter is great on barbecued chops or hamburgers. Perk up egg salad sandwiches with a little lemon thyme. Add thyme to fish stuffings, poultry stuffings, beef-stock marinades and veal stew. Thyme vinegar has a clean flavor and looks beautiful with a bay leaf and a clove of garlic added to the bottle. Lemon thyme tea is a refreshing pick-me-up. It is a versatile, year-round herb.

Growing

A shrubby perennial, thyme is another large group of plants with confusing names. We grow a broad-leafed thyme, known as common or English thyme, and lemon thyme. The more upright varieties are best for culinary uses. Thyme needs a light, limy, moderately fertile soil and good drainage. Plants are propagated by seed (except lemon thyme), cuttings, layering or division of the whole plant. When layering or dividing plants, the woody portions of the stem should be buried. After three to four years, plants get very woody and produce fewer leaves. This is when they should be divided. Thyme makes an attractive container plant, but watering can be a problem in the winter. In general, it is best to keep plants on the dry side. The cooler the temperature, the less water thyme needs.

Pot Roast with Thyme

To be working in the garden while a thyme-scented pot roast simmers away in the kitchen—this is a very pleasant prospect indeed for the cook and gardener. Serve this roast with mashed potatoes and a green vegetable. Serves 4-6.

3-lb. (1.5-kg) beef chuck roast

flour for dredging

freshly ground black pepper

4-5 Tbsp. (60-75 mL) vegetable oil

1 medium onion, chopped

2 cloves garlic, peeled and crushed

2 cups (500 mL) beef stock

1 5 1/2-oz. (156-mL) can tomato paste

3 Tbsp. (45 mL) finely chopped thyme

Preheat oven to 325°F (160°C). Put flour on a plate and season with pepper. Dredge roast in flour. Heat oil in a Dutch oven and sauté roast on all sides until browned. Remove roast from Dutch oven and set aside. Sauté onion and garlic in Dutch oven for 3-4 minutes until browned. Remove Dutch oven from heat.

Mix beef stock, tomato paste and thyme together in a blender or food processor. Return roast to Dutch oven. Pour stock mixture over roast and bring to a boil. Cover and bake in preheated oven for 2 hours. Test for doneness. Meat should be tender and easy to carve. Bake longer if necessary.

When roast is done, skim fat from pan and thicken pan juices, if desired. Slice roast and pour pan juices over top.

French Onion Soup with Thyme

One of the chefs who buys herbs from us told us that the secret of his French onion soup is our lemon thyme. The herb, and the long, slow cooking process, accounts for the wonderful flavor of this soup. Serves 4.

4-5 medium onions, thinly sliced

1 Tbsp. (15 mL) butter

1 Tbsp. (15 mL) vegetable oil

1 tsp. (5 mL) sugar

3 cups (750 mL) beef stock

1/4 cup (50 mL) dry red wine

3 Tbsp. (45 mL) finely chopped lemon thyme

freshly ground black pepper

4 slices toasted French bread

2 cups (500 mL) freshly grated Gruyre cheese

In a heavy-bottomed saucepan, cook onions in butter and oil over medium heat for 15 minutes. Cover saucepan while cooking and stir occasionally to prevent onions sticking. Remove half the onions from saucepan and set aside. Add sugar to remaining onions and cook for an additional 30 minutes, stirring often. Onions should be a deep golden color.

Add beef stock and wine to saucepan and simmer for 40 minutes. Return first half of onions to saucepan, add thyme, season with pepper and heat through. To serve, ladle into ovenproof soup bowls and put a slice of toasted French bread in each bowl. Cover bread with cheese and broil/grill briefly until cheese has browned. Serve immediately.

Steamed Clams with Lemon Thyme Butter

This can be a first course or a main dish. The clam nectar, perfumed with lemon thyme, makes a superb hot drink, or you can use it later for fish stock. Serve the clams with a loaf of crusty bread. Serves 4.

4-6 lbs. (2-3 kg) fresh clams, washed and scrubbed

1/2 cup (125 mL) cold water

1 cup (250 mL) Lemon Thyme Butter (recipe follows)

Put clams and water in a pot, cover and steam clams for 5-6 minutes until their shells open. Drain, reserving liquid for other uses. Strain liquid through a sieve lined with a linen or muslin cloth and set aside. Leave clams in shells. Discard any clams that do not open. Put clams in soup bowls and serve with individual bowls of Lemon Thyme Butter.

Lemon Thyme Butter

1 cup (250 mL) butter

juice of 1 lemon

1 Tbsp. (15 mL) finely chopped lemon thyme

Melt butter in a saucepan. Add lemon juice and blend in. Add lemon thyme and mix together.

Creole Baked Cod with Thyme

How much "Creole" you want with the cod depends on the cook.
Increase the hot-pepper sauce, garlic and pepper if you wish.
Serves 4.

2 cups (500 mL) sliced onions

1 cup (250 mL) sliced mushrooms

2 green bell peppers, seeded and cut in strips

2 cloves garlic, peeled and crushed

2-3 Tbsp. (30-45 mL) olive oil

3 tomatoes, peeled and chopped

2 Tbsp. (30 mL) finely chopped thyme

1 bay leaf

dash of hot-pepper sauce

freshly ground black pepper

4 cod steaks, approximately 1 inch (2.5 cm) thick

Preheat oven to 450°F (230°C). Sauté onions, mushrooms, peppers and garlic in oil in a skillet until onions are limp. Add tomatoes, thyme, bay leaf and hot-pepper sauce to skillet and simmer over medium heat for 10 minutes. Season with pepper. Put cod steaks in a baking dish and pour vegetables over top. Cover and bake in preheated oven for 15 minutes or until done. To serve, spoon vegetables over cod steaks and use pan juices as a sauce.

Beef Stew with Beer and Thyme

Beer makes a good, rich stock for beef stews, as the Dutch have taught us. The yeasty beer flavor adds another taste dimension to the herbed gravy. Potatoes, carrots and mushrooms may be added to this stew during the last hour of cooking. Serve it on its own or over hot noodles. Serves 4-6.

2 lbs. (1 kg) stewing beef, cut in bite-sized pieces, with the
   fat removed

1/4 cup (50 mL) flour

3-4 Tbsp. (45-60 mL) vegetable oil

2 medium onions, finely chopped

2 cups (500 mL) dark beer or stout

2 Tbsp. (30 mL) finely chopped thyme

2 Tbsp. (30 mL) finely chopped parsley

freshly ground black pepper

Preheat oven to 350°F (180°C). Put flour on a plate, and dredge beef in flour, shaking off the excess. Sauté beef in oil in a skillet for 3 minutes until lightly browned. Put beef in an ovenproof casserole dish.

Add onion to skillet and sauté until lightly browned. Add beer or stout, thyme and parsley to skillet and bring to a boil. Season with pepper. Transfer contents of skillet to casserole dish. Bake in preheated oven for 2 hours or until beef is tender.

Calf Liver Cooked in Wine with Thyme

The red wine makes a light rosy sauce that is a good contrast to the rich taste of the liver. Even those who are not fans of liver have been known to admit that this dish is good! Serves 2.

1 large onion, thinly sliced

3-4 Tbsp. (45-60 mL) vegetable oil

1/4 cup (50 mL) flour

3/4 lb. (350 g) calf liver, very thinly sliced

1/2 cup (125 mL) dry red wine

1 Tbsp. (15 mL) finely chopped thyme

freshly ground black pepper

Sauté onion in oil in a skillet for 2-3 minutes until limp. Remove onion from skillet and set aside. Put flour on a plate and dust liver in flour. Sauté liver in skillet over high heat for 1 minute per side. Return onion to skillet, add wine and thyme and continue to cook over high heat for 1 minute. Season with pepper. The wine sauce should thicken. Stir so that the liver does not stick to skillet. Serve immediately with sauce over top.

Bouquet Garni

A bouquet garni can be made from fresh or dried herbs. It makes a delightful gift for friends who like to cook. It is used in soups, stocks, stews and in poaching fish. The traditional bouquet garni consists of thyme, bay leaf and parsley, but it can also be made with basil, chervil, rosemary, savory or tarragon.

Tie a thread around the herbs you have selected and you have a bouquet garni. It is always removed from the dish before it is served. For a dried herbal bouquet, stitch herbs in a cheesecloth bag and dry them on a rack in a dust-free and dry-ventilated room.

Herbal Desserts
& Sweet Herbal Baking

*W*hen I first began to cook with fresh herbs I did not think much about using herbs in desserts or in cakes and cookies. Occasionally I flung some mint leaves onto a dish of ice cream, but the serious use of herbs in or on desserts began when I started giving herbal lunch and dinner classes at the farm. I could not possibly serve a dessert without some kind of herb in it, and so my search for recipes and experimentation began.

The recipes I found mainly used mints, lemon verbena, lemon balm, lemon thyme, sweet cicely and angelica. These herbs were perfect for desserts: their sprightly flavors combined well with citrus juice and citrus rind, enlivening custards, sorbets, ice cream, cakes and cookies.

Here is a small selection of herbal desserts that I have developed over the years. I hope they will encourage you to go on and experiment with your own combinations. Use your old favorite recipes, and add herbs to create new culinary discoveries. For extra inspiration, *Cooking With Flowers*, by Jenny Leggat, is a most beautiful book about using flowers and herbs in desserts.

Puréed Summer Fruit with Lemon Balm

The first summer apples on our herb farm come from an ancient apple tree that was planted many years ago. The sheep stand under the tree waiting for the apples to fall. The apples and blackberries are ripe at the same time, which makes for an interesting coincidence. We cook apples and blackberries together and add lemon balm. Put a dollop of this summer fruit mixture on your morning cereal, or serve with ice cream. Lemon balm can also be added to apple sauce. Serves 4-6.

6-8 early-ripening apples, peeled, cored and sliced

3-4 cups (750 mL-1 L) ripe blackberries

1/4 cup (50 mL) sugar (optional)

1/4 cup (50 mL) finely chopped lemon balm

1 cup (250 mL) or less cold water

Mix all ingredients together in a saucepan and bring to a boil. Reduce heat to low, cover and simmer for 10 to 15 minutes until fruit is cooked. Cool and serve, or chill in the refrigerator until ready to serve.

Lemon Balm-Yogurt Dessert Sauce

This is a handy sauce to have on hand during the fresh fruit season. Use on fruit salad, peaches, raspberries, strawberries or blackberries. Makes 2 cups (500 mL).

1 1/2 cups (375 mL) yogurt

2 Tbsp. (30 mL) freshly squeezed lemon juice

4 Tbsp. (60 mL) sugar

1/4 cup (50 mL) finely chopped lemon balm

Mix ingredients in a bowl and chill in refrigerator for a few hours before serving. The flavors will blend and increase.

Poached Fruit with Wine and Lemon Balm

This is a very adaptable recipe: as the summer fruit ripens you can just switch the fruit. I have used apricots, apples, peaches and pears—and sometimes a mixture. Serves 2-4.

2 cups (500 mL) white wine

1 cup (250 mL) finely chopped lemon balm

4 apples, peeled and sliced, or 2 cups (500 mL)
   other fruit in season

1 lemon, thinly sliced

1/2 cup (125 mL) whipped cream or yogurt

lemon balm leaves, as garnish

Heat the white wine with the lemon balm until it is just boiling. Add the fruit and poach it for about 10 minutes or until it is just tender. Put into a serving bowl and add sliced lemon. Refrigerate. Serve with a dollop of whipped cream or yogurt. Decorate with some lemon balm leaves.

Lemon-Herbed White Port Sorbet

Tart with lemony herbs and lemons, this sorbet is refreshing after a rich meal. To increase the flavor intensity, make the herb-flavored sugar syrup and refrigerate overnight or longer before making the sorbet. Serves 6.

2 cups (500 mL) sugar

2 cups (500 mL) water

2 cups (500 mL) chopped mint, lemon verbena and
lemon balm (mix and match the herbs depending on
what you have growing in the garden)

2 cups (500 mL) white port or white wine

1 1/2 cups (375 mL) fresh orange juice

1 cup (250 mL) freshly squeezed lemon juice

3 Tbsp. (45 mL) grated lemon zest

thin slices of lemon, and mint or lemon balm leaves, as garnish

Place sugar, water and chopped herbs in a saucepan and bring to a boil. Simmer gently for 5 minutes. Refrigerate overnight.

To make the sorbet, stir the herb syrup, wine, orange juice, lemon juice and lemon zest together in a bowl. Freeze in an ice-cream maker or in ice-cube trays. Remove from freezer about 15 minutes before serving so you can scoop it out easily. Serve in glass bowls or wine glasses, and decorate with mint or lemon balm leaves and thin slices of lemon.

Mint Sorbet

Try this light and enticing dessert after a rich meal, or serve it after the main course to refresh the palate, as they do in France. This recipe can be made with an ice-cream maker if you have one. Serves 4.

1/4 cup (50 mL) sugar

1 1/2 cups (375 mL) boiling water

1 cup (250 mL) mint leaves

juice of 1 lemon, orange or lime

2 egg whites

thin lemon slices and mint sprigs, as garnish

mint liqueur (optional)

Dissolve sugar in boiling water in a saucepan. Add mint and set aside for 30 minutes. The longer you leave the mixture, the stronger the flavor will be. Taste and decide what strength you would like. When it is the strength you like, strain and discard mint.

Add lemon, orange or lime juice to saucepan and stir. Pour contents of saucepan into a container and freeze for 1 hour, until slushy.

Beat egg whites in a bowl until stiff. Remove container from freezer and fold egg whites into frozen mint mixture. Return container to freezer for at least 1 hour. Spoon mixture into sorbet glasses. Garnish each glass with a thin slice of lemon and a sprig of mint. If desired, splash a small amount of mint liqueur over each sorbet. Serve immediately.

Lemony Lemon Balm Custard

When I make this custard from eggs provided by my free-range hens, the yellow color is extraordinary. The flavor is very intense. Sometimes I substitute mint for the lemon balm. Serves 6.

12 egg yolks

1 1/2 cups (375 mL) dry white wine

1/2 cup (125 mL) chopped lemon balm or mint

3/4 cup (175 mL) fresh lemon juice

2/3 cup (170 mL) sugar

lemon balm or mint sprigs, as garnish

Beat yolks, wine, lemon balm, lemon juice and sugar together in the top of a double boiler until the mixture is thick. This takes about 15 minutes. Sieve the custard and discard the lemon balm leaves. Pour into small glass bowls and chill. Garnish with lemon balm or mint leaves, or flowers, such as violets or English daisies.

Basil Ice Cream with Bitter Chocolate Sauce

In one of my cooking classes the theme was a basil and garlic dinner. I searched and searched for a basil dessert, for I had decided against a garlic one. I found this basil ice cream in a cookbook called The Natural Cuisine of Georges Blanc, *by Georges Blanc, a famous French chef in Burgundy. It has an amazing, spicy, exotic flavor. I devised the bitter chocolate sauce for a topping; it makes a good contrast to the basil. Serves 4.*

2 cups (500 mL) milk

1/2 vanilla bean

1 cup (250 mL) basil leaves

4 egg yolks

1 cup (250 mL) sugar

Bitter Chocolate Sauce (recipe follows)

Bring milk, vanilla bean and basil to a boil in a medium saucepan. Remove from heat, cover and let steep for 10 to 15 minutes.

In a large bowl, whisk the egg yolks and sugar until thick and creamy. Strain milk to remove basil and vanilla bean. Pour milk into egg and sugar mixture. Whisk well, pour into saucepan and cook over low heat. Stir constantly with a wooden spoon for 5 to 7 minutes. Cool. Freeze in an ice-cream maker according to directions. Serve with chocolate sauce on top.

Bitter Chocolate Sauce

This recipe keeps well in the refrigerator and can be made ahead of time. Makes 1 cup (250 mL).

4 oz. (110 g) unsweetened chocolate

2 Tbsp. (30 mL) butter

2 Tbsp. (30 mL) white corn syrup

3/4 cup (175 mL) milk

6-8 Tbsp. (90-120 mL) sugar

1/4 tsp. (1.25 mL) salt

Melt chocolate with butter in a double boiler. Add corn syrup and blend with a spoon. Add milk, sugar and salt. Cook while stirring over low heat for 10 minutes. Serve warm or cool over ice cream.

Minted Chocolate Mousse

This mousse can be made the day before a dinner party. The combination of mint, liqueur, coffee and chocolate produces a rich, complex flavor. Serves 4-6.

1/2 cup (125 mL) chocolate chips

3 Tbsp. (45 mL) black coffee

2 Tbsp. (30 mL) crème de menthe or a coffee liqueur

4 large eggs, separated

2 Tbsp. (30 mL) very finely chopped mint leaves

sprigs of mint for decoration

In a heavy-bottomed pot or double boiler, melt the chocolate. Whisk in the coffee and liqueur until smooth. Remove from heat and whisk in the egg yolks one at a time. Stir in the chopped mint.

In a separate bowl, beat the egg whites until stiff. Fold into the chocolate mixture. Spoon into small dessert cups and refrigerate. Top with sprigs of mint before serving.

Lemon Meringue Pie with Lemon Balm

Use your regular lemon meringue pie recipe, and add 1 Tbsp. (15 mL) finely chopped lemon balm, or cook the lemon custard with 5-6 whole lemon balm leaves and strain them out later. After the meringue is baked, decorate top of pie with lemon balm leaves.

Lemon Balm Cookies

These cookies have faint green specks and are delicious served with ice cream or custard. Makes about 16 small cookies.

1/2 cup (125 mL) butter

1/2 cup (125 mL) white sugar

1 egg, beaten

2 cups (500 mL) all-purpose flour

1/4 cup (50 mL) finely chopped lemon balm

Cream butter and sugar. Add egg, flour and lemon balm mix until the dough is firm. Wrap in plastic wrap and chill for 1 hour.

Roll out the dough on a lightly floured surface. Cut cookies with a pastry cutter. Place on a greased baking sheet for 10 to 12 minutes at 350°F (175°C). They should just be turning brown at the edges. Cool on a rack.

Rosemary-Thyme Shortbread

I found the source of this recipe in a Brooklyn Botanical Garden herb book and it was a summer hit served with sorbets. Serve the cookies on a plate decorated with sprigs of rosemary and lemon thyme. Makes about 30 cookies.

1/4 cup (50 mL) icing sugar

9 Tbsp. (135 mL) soft butter

1 1/2 cups (375 mL) all-purpose flour

1 Tbsp. (15 mL) finely chopped fresh rosemary

1 Tbsp. (15 mL) finely chopped lemon thyme

1 Tbsp. (15 mL) granulated sugar

Preheat oven to 350°F (175°C). Combine the icing sugar and butter and mix well. Stir in the flour, rosemary and thyme. Knead the dough a few times on a lightly floured surface. Roll out the dough to about 1/4-inch (1/2-cm) thickness and cut into shapes. Bake on a greased cookie sheet until cookies are a pale gold color. Sprinkle granulated sugar on the cookies and cool on racks. Store in an airtight tin.

Lemon Thyme Cake

This loaf cake was a hit at a herbal tea and tour of the garden. It keeps well and also freezes well. The lemon glaze adds extra lemon punch. Makes about 12 slices.

2 cups (500 mL) unbleached flour

2 tsp. (10 mL) baking powder

sprinkle of salt

6 Tbsp. (90 mL) softened butter

1 cup (250 mL) sugar

2 eggs

1 Tbsp. (15 mL) grated lemon zest

2 Tbsp. (30 mL) fresh lemon juice

2 Tbsp. (30 mL) chopped lemon thyme

2/3 cup (170 mL) milk

2 Tbsp. (30 mL) fresh lemon juice

1/2 cup (125 mL) icing sugar

Preheat oven to 325°F (160°C). Grease and flour a loaf pan.

Sift together flour, baking powder and salt. In another bowl, cream the butter and beat in the sugar until fluffy. Add eggs and beat well. Stir in lemon zest, 2 Tbsp. (30 mL) lemon juice, lemon thyme and milk. Slowly whisk in the flour mixture and mix well.

Pour into the loaf pan. Bake for 1 hour, or until a knife inserted comes out clean. Cool on a rack.

To make the lemon glaze, mix 2 Tbsp. (30 mL) lemon juice with the icing sugar so it is of a thin pourable consistency. Pour over the cooled cake, spread with a brush, and serve.

Blackberry Mint Muffins

I like to make these muffins in August, when the blackberries and mint are flourishing, but you can make them in winter if you have some frozen berries and a bag of frozen mint. Makes 12 muffins.

1 1/2 cups (375 mL) fresh blackberries

1/2 cup (125 mL) finely chopped mint

1 cup (250 mL) sunflower seeds

2 cups (500 mL) all-purpose flour

1 Tbsp. (15 mL) baking powder

3/4 cup (175 mL) brown sugar

1/2 cup (125 mL) buttermilk

1/3 cup (75 mL) vegetable oil

1 egg

Preheat oven to 400°F (200°C). Grease a muffin tin. Mix together the blackberries, mint and sunflower seeds. In a larger bowl, mix the flour, baking powder and sugar. In another bowl, mix buttermilk, oil and egg together. Pour the liquid mixture into the flour mixture and mix until just blended. Fold the blackberry-mint mixture into the batter until just mixed. Spoon into muffin cups and bake for 20 to 25 minutes. Cool on a rack.

Bibliography

Belsinger, Susan and Carolyn Dille. *Cooking with Herbs*. New York: Van Nostrand Reinhold, 1984.

Boxer, Arabella and P. Back. *The Herb Book*. London: Octopus Books, 1980.

Crockett, James and Ogden Tanner. *Herbs*. Alexandria, Virginia: Time-life Encyclopedia of Gardening, Time-Life Books Inc., 1977.

Edinger, Philip, ed. *How to Grow Herbs*. Menlo Park, California: Sunset Books, 1984.

Foley, Daniel, ed. *Herbs for Use and Delight*. New York: Dover Publications Inc., 1974.

Garland, Sarah. *The Herb Garden*. New York: Viking-Penguin, 1984.

Hampstead, Marilyn. *The Basil Book*. New York: Long Shadow Books, Pocket Books, 1984.

Hemphill, Rosemary. *Herbs for All Seasons*. Harmondsworth, England: Penguin Books, 1975.

Holt, Geraldine. *Recipes From a French Herb Garden*. London: Stoddart, 1989.

Howarth, Sheila. *Herbs with Everything*. London: Sphere Books, 1977.

Jacobs, E.M. Betty. *Growing and Using Herbs Successfully*. Vermont: Garden Way, 1976.

McGourty, F., ed. *Handbook on Herbs*. Brooklyn, New York: Brooklyn Botanic Garden, 1977.

Norman, Jill. *Salad Herbs*. New York: Bantam, 1989.

Page, Mary and W.T. Stern. *Culinary Herbs*. London: Wisley Handbook No. 16, The Royal Horticulture Society, 1980.

Peplow, Elizabeth and Reginald. *Herbs and Herb Gardens of Britain*. Exeter, England: Webb and Bower, 1984.

Simmons, Adele G. *Herb Gardens of Delight*. New York: Hawthorne Books, 1974.

_____. *A Merry Christmas Herbal*. New York: William Morrow, 1968.

Sunset Books, ed. *Gardening in Containers*. Menlo Park, California: Sunset Books, 1959.

Tolley, Emelie and Chris Mead. *Herbs, Gardens, Decorations and Recipes*. New York: Clarkson N. Potter, 1985.

Van Brunt, ed. *Handbook on Culinary Herbs*. Brooklyn, New York: Brooklyn Botanic Garden, 1982.

Seed & Plant Sources

From April through June, one can usually find small herb plants for sale at most local nurseries. The following is a list of herb seed and plant sources.

Abundant Life Seeds, Box 772, Port Townsend, Washington, U.S.A. 98368; (206) 385-5660. Extensive Catalogue of herb, vegetable and flower seeds. Also gardening and philosophical advice.

Bagga Pasta Ltd., #4 - 1516 Fairfield Road, Victoria, B.C., V8S 1G1; (604) 598-1153; or ¹04 - 2000 Cadboro Bay, Victoria, B.C., V8R 5G5; (604) 598-7575. Fresh herbs, vinegars, mustards, fresh pasta cookbooks.

Cedarbrook Herb Farm, 986 Sequim Avenue, South Sequim, Washington, U.S.A. 98382; (206) 683-7733. Tony and Terry Anderson.

Cobble Hill Herb Farm, 3025 Cobble Hill Road, Cobble Hill, B.C., V0R 1L0; (604) 743-3094. Mabel and Forbes Abercrombie. Plants, seeds and herbal gifts for sale.

The Cook's Garden, Box 65, Londonderry, Vermont, U.S.A. 05148; (802) 824-3400. Catalogue containing exotic salad greens and culinary herbs.

Dacha Barinka, 46232 Strathcona Road, Chilliwack, B.C., V2P 3T2. Catalogue of interesting vegetable, flower and herb seeds.

Dig This Gifts and Gear For Gardeners, 45 Bastion Square, Victoria, B.C., V8W 1J1; (604) 385-3212. Herb seeds and plants.

Elk Lake Garden Centre, 5450 Patricia Bay Hwy., Victoria, B.C., V8Y 1T1; (604) 658-8812. Herb seeds and plants.

Foxglove Herb Farm, 6617 Rosedale Street, Gig Harbor, Washington, U.S.A. 98335; (206) 851-8782. Michael Burkhardt.

Happy Valley Herb Farm, 3497 Happy Valley Road, Victoria, B.C., V9C 2X2; (604) 474-5767. Lynda and Mike Dowling. Herb plants, dried flowers, potpourris, fresh and dry herbs, herbal workshops. Open April to September.

Havasu Hills Herb Farm, 3717 Stoney Road, Coulterville, California, U.S.A. 95311; (209) 878-3102. Herb plants.

Hazelwood Farm, 13576 Adshead Road, R.R. #1, Ladysmith, B.C., V0R 2E0; (604) 245-8007. Richard White and Jaycynthe Dugas. Herb plants.

Herb Gathering Inc., 5742 Kenwood Avenue, Kansas City, Missouri, U.S.A. 64110. Catalogue of French vegetables and herbs.

Les Herbes Fines de Sainte-Antoine, 480 Chemin l'Acadie, Sainte-Antoine-sur-Richilieu, Quebec, J0L 1R0. Selection of hardy herb seeds and scented geraniums.

The Herbfarm, 32804 Issaquah, Fall City Road, Fall City, Washington, U.S.A. 98024; (206) 784-2222. Over 400 varieties of herb plants; gift shop, gardens, school and restaurant. Free catalogue of classes and products.

Island Seed, Box 4278, Station A, Victoria, B.C., V8X 3X8; (604) 479-3170. Mail-order catalogue of herb, flower and vegetable seeds. Seeds are also available in British Columbia garden centers.

Le Jardin du Gourmet, West Danville, Vermont, U.S.A. 05873. Garlic, shallots, herb seedlings; vegetable and herb seeds. Free catalogue.

Lowland Herb Farm, Box 255, Sardis, B.C., V2R 1A6; (604) 858-4216. Fresh herbs, salad herbs and edible plants; herb plants. Please telephone first.

Nichol's Herbs and Rare Seeds, Nichol's Garden Nursery, 1190 North Pacific Highway, Albany, Oregon, U.S.A. 97321; (503) 928-9280. Catalogue of herb seeds.

Ravenhill Herb Farm, 1330 Mt. Newton Crossroad, R.R. #2, Saanichton, B.C., V0S 1M0; (604) 652-4024. Noël Richardson and Andrew Yeoman. Herb farm; herb plants and herb books. Open Sundays, April through August, 12:00 to 5:00 p.m.

Richter's, Goodwood, Ontario, L0C 1A0; (416) 640-6677. Extensive annotated herb catalogue that contains seeds, plants, books and herbal gifts.

Sanctuary Seeds/Folklore Herbs, 2388 West 4th Avenue, Vancouver, B.C., V6K 1P1; (604) 733-4724. Free catalogue.

Shepherd's Garden Seeds, Shipping Office, 30 Irene Street, Torrington, Connecticut, U.S.A. 06790; (203) 482-3638; or 7389 West Zayonte Road, Felton, California, U.S.A. 95018; (408) 335-5400. Herb, flower and vegetable seeds.

Territorial Seed Company, Box 27, 80030 Territorial Road, Lorane, Oregon, U.S.A. 97451; (503) 942-9547. Catalogue of vegetable and herb seeds that grow well in coastal climates. Good cultivation advice.

Index